NEURONS
Building Blocks of the Brain

BY THE AUTHOR

NEURONS
Building Blocks of the Brain

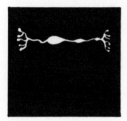

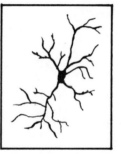

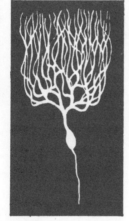

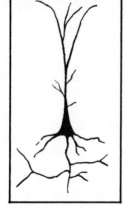

Leonard A. Stevens
Illustrated by Henry Roth

THOMAS Y. CROWELL COMPANY • NEW YORK

Thanks are due to the American Association for the Advancement of Science for the illustration on page 64 (copyright © 1966 by the American Association for the Advancement of Science) and to the National Aeronautics and Space Administration for the photograph used on page 70.

Library of Congress Cataloging in Publication Data
Stevens, Leonard A. Neurons: building blocks of the brain. SUMMARY: Traces the history of research on the nervous system and discusses what has been learned about the structure, function, and importance of neurons or nerve cells. Bibliography: p.   1. Neurons—Juv. lit. 2. Brain—Juv. lit. 3. Neural transmission—Juv. lit. [1. Neurons. 2. Brain.   3.   Nervous   system]   I.   Roth,   Henry,   1933–   illus.   II.   Title. QP363.S783   591.1'88   74-4399   ISBN 0-690-00403-6

1   2   3   4   5   6   7   8   9   10

Contents

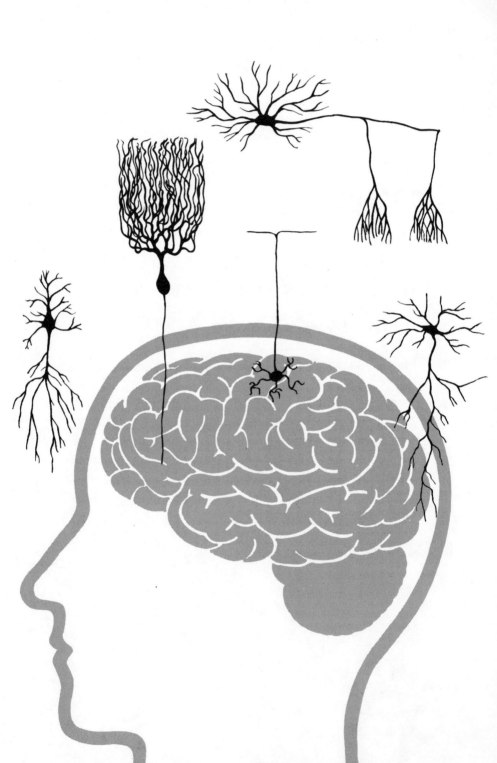

Some principal neuron cell types of the human brain.

1 The Neuron: The Key to Life and Thought

OF ALL THE living organs the brain is by far the most important for human existence. As the dominant part of the nervous system the brain is the powerful, mysterious master of life and thought, and all the other organs are its servants. The magnificent mysteries of this complex gelatinous mass embedded in our heads have been the objects of the longest, greatest exploration of all time—the struggle of man's brain to understand itself. The answers to these mysteries are locked tightly into the basic building blocks of the nervous system—the neurons.

A neuron is a nerve cell. It is, with little question, the most interesting, most important cell in living organisms. It is in the weave of intricate tissue that forms both the central nervous system (brain and spinal cord) and peripheral nerves connecting the central system with muscles and glands throughout the body. On the one hand the cell makes up the "motor" controls, the part of the nervous system that reaches out to muscles and determines our physical movements. The neuron is also the basic unit of our five senses—sight, hearing, smell, taste, and feeling— and such less known senses as those that tell us the position of an arm or leg without looking at it. Also, the neuron is the cell responsible for that most fantastic but mysterious of all living phenomena: memory. How we remember and forget has yet to be explained. Undoubtedly the answer is to be found within the neurons.

In short, the study of the neuron comes ever so close to some of the oldest, most important questions of all time: Who are we? How do we relate to the world around us? In the neuron we

1

stand to learn the physical facts of how, on the one hand, we can enjoy the beauties of a spring morning, yet become enraged enough in the same day to kill another human being. Somewhere in the neurons are answers to the difficult questions of what happens in the brain when learning takes place. Many theories have been advanced, but they have not been fully supported by evidence of physical changes that could explain the learning process. The evidence still remains hidden somewhere in the nerve cells.

The study of the neuron is also the way toward understanding some of humankind's most devastating diseases. When the nervous system fails, it can cripple an individual by damaging the motor controls that guide his muscles. Disorders of the nervous system can rob a person of speech, vision, or hearing, cutting him off from his fellow men. They can spoil the ability to learn, and thus leave a person mentally dependent on others around him. They are disorders that often change the very nature of the afflicted person. While one might suffer diseases of the heart, liver, or other organs, he would still retain the personality that characterized him. But a disorder of the nervous system might actually change the human qualities that determine that personality. He would no longer be himself.

These problems are more perplexing because the neuron, unlike other cells, does not reproduce. It has but one life. At birth the human brain arrives with its full, lifelong supply of nerve cells, some twelve billion, and any that are lost through disease, physical damage, or aging, are never restored. So, very often, the brain, spinal cord, or a nerve that malfunctions because of loss of nerve cells may be a permanent affliction. Then the only hope may lie in the lost functions being taken over by the healthy cells among the billions that remain.

In any event, the science of the neurons holds the hope of learning about ourselves in love and violence, in serenity and worry, and in health and illnesses. But the infinitely small size of

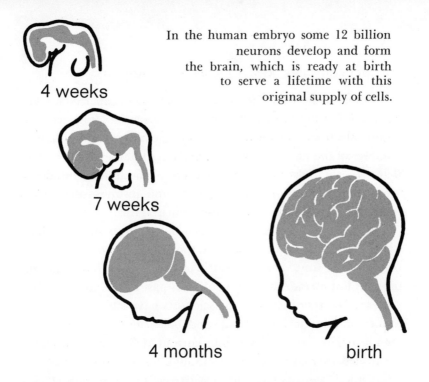

In the human embryo some 12 billion neurons develop and form the brain, which is ready at birth to serve a lifetime with this original supply of cells.

4 weeks

7 weeks

4 months

birth

the neuron is a barrier to understanding it. The tiny dimensions are evident when it is revealed that the brain's twelve billion nerve cells are packed into the skull with several times that number of another type of cell, the glial cell. Even in the human body a single nerve bundle, much thinner than a hair, may consist of 100,000 fibers called *axons,* each an extension of only a single nerve cell.

Yet the neuron, despite its extremely small size, is a very complex electrical unit. In action a nerve cell transmits a wave of electrical current, a *nerve impulse.* It moves along the cell's single axon to another neuron, or to a muscle or gland. The junction between neurons is called a *synapse,* which means to clasp, but we now know that in most cases nerve cells do not quite come together. They are separated at the synapse by an unimaginably fine gap, the *synaptic cleft.* We have also learned that when an impulse is transmitted across the typical synapse, it is actually accomplished by the electricity starting a chemical action that occurs in the synaptic cleft.

3

Some of the most fascinating, provocative experiments and discoveries in the history of science have been involved, with the minute electrical-chemical activities of the billions and billions of synapses of the nervous system. They have often evoked the idea that even the most intangible qualities of the human mind and soul—such as memory, forgetfulness, and instinct—may eventually be explained in electrical-chemical terms.

For example, brain scientists who are also surgeons have stimulated certain minute areas in the brains of conscious human beings with tiny, gentle electric currents and have literally brought lost memories from the distant past to the minds of their patients. In other instances the scientists have actually been able to turn on or off feelings of rage and violence in a human patient by turning on and off a feeble current delivered by ultrafine electrodes inserted in the brain through holes in the skull.

Other scientists have devoted careers to study the electrical patterns of the brain's billions of neurons, and they have recognized that everything from the blink of an eye to the solution of difficult problems in calculus has an impact on these patterns. The electrical activity of the brain, which never ceases between the early beginnings of life of the fetus in a mother's womb to the moment of death, can tell the expert a great deal about the functionings of the brain. Damage to the organ from disease or physical violence may be diagnosed by the changes it causes in the brain's ongoing electrical activity. Scientists have also learned a lot about the nature of sleep by observing the electrical patterns from the brains of slumbering subjects.

For centuries people have futilely tried to fathom what happens in the brain when a memory is lodged in the gray matter. Modern brain scientists have finally begun turning up evidence indicating that in learning something, a brain actually experiences physical changes. Some highly provocative experiments on animal brains in recent years have indicated that in trained, compared to untrained, animals there is a difference in the neurons and their chemicals. Some of the most controversial experiments of the entire science of the nervous system have proposed that memories may be transferable from one brain to another by transferring certain chemicals from a trained to an untrained brain.

These and other fascinating studies of the nervous system, which will be covered in forthcoming chapters, always come back to that basic building block of conscious life and thought: the neuron. But throughout most of recorded history this key cell of all cells was unknown, and the brain, spinal cord, and nerves were far more mysterious than today. The story of man's brain trying to understand itself goes back several centuries before Christ, but the most substantial discoveries, closely related to recognition of the neuron, came only in the past few centuries.

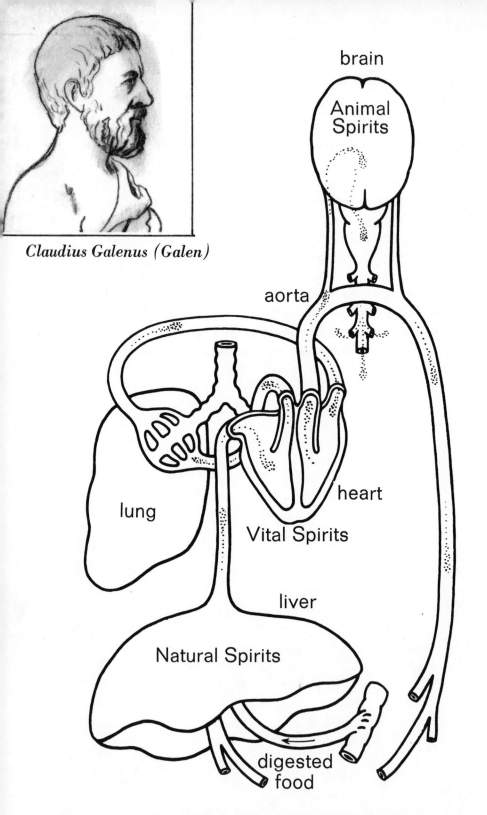

Claudius Galenus (Galen)

brain

Animal
Spirits

aorta

lung

heart

Vital Spirits

liver

Natural Spirits

digested
food

Galen's concept of how the nervous system worked.

2 The Long Life of Animal Spirits

In THE 1730s an unusual electrical experiment was performed in Europe by an Englishman, Stephen Gray, whose subject was a young boy suspended horizontally on two ropes so that his nose was very close to an electroscope, a device for detecting static electricity. When Gray generated a static charge by rubbing a glass tube with a soft cloth, he could transfer it to the boy through his feet and the youngster's nose would then deflect the electroscope. The experiment revealed that the boy's body, like the rod, could hold an electrical charge.

It was a dramatic stunt with little meaning for biology, but it indicated how men were thinking that life and electricity might be related. Scientists had agreed long ago that some mysterious force prompted and controlled muscular activities in animals and humans. Indeed, the force had been given a name by a famous physician who lived about a century after the time of Christ.

This great doctor, Claudius Galenus (Galen) was born about 130 A.D. in the ancient city of Pergamum (now Bergama, Turkey). His father, an architect, had supposedly been visited in a dream by Aesculapius, the god of medicine, and told that his son should become a physician. Galen became one of the most famous doctors in the entire history of medicine. He eventually settled in Rome as court physician to Emperor Marcus Aurelius. However, Galen's most important work was in anatomy, and his studies included the nervous system. He, in fact, developed a surprisingly clear idea of how the system works. Galen decided that nerves could be generally classified as belonging to two pathways. One was related to the senses and the other to muscular movements (eventually they truly became known as the sensory and motor pathways).

The famous physician found some good evidence for his double-pathway idea in a patient, Pausania. The man had injured his spinal cord in a fall from a chariot, and he had suffered the loss of feeling in the fingers of one hand, although he could still move them. Galen concluded that only the sensory pathway had been damaged, leaving the motor nerves to function as usual.

He strengthened his theory with some experimental work on the spinal cords of living animals. Galen surgically cut part-way through the cords and found that he could reproduce the kind of damage seen in Pausania. A creature's sense of feeling could be taken away from certain areas of its body by severing a certain part of its cord, yet its ability to move would remain unchanged. Or vice versa, the ability to move could be damaged (leaving the sense of feeling) with incisions across other parts of the cord.

Obviously some kind of force was moving through the spinal cord and the body's tiny nerves leading out to the muscles. Galen, who wrongly concluded the nerves were tiny hollow tubes, decided they were carrying ethereal (light, airy) spirits, which he called "animal spirits." He believed that they originated in cavities of the brain known as ventricles. In fact, Galen worked out an entire process to explain the making of animal spirits. He decided that digested food was transferred to the liver and turned into "natural spirits." They flowed to the heart to become "vital spirits." Finally the blood carried vital spirits to the brain for transformation to animal spirits to be used in the nervous system.

The idea was not easily disproven, and it remained in force for centuries. Many of the world's greatest thinkers accepted animal spirits as the nerve force. For example, in the seventeenth century the famous French philosopher, mathematician, and scientist, René Descartes, advanced some new ideas about brains and nerves, but he did not question Galen's animal spirits.

Thomas Willis, an English physician who lived in Descartes's time, also made some important observations about nervous functions, but he didn't contest Galen's idea. Willis noted that shutting off the blood flow from the heart to the brain also put an end to nervous activity. He felt it was simply a matter of vital spirits being blocked in their passage from the heart to the brain for conversion into the crucial animal spirits. The English physician, working with animals, also found that he could paralyze a limb by tightly binding the nerves leading to it. Again the answer seemed simple: the binding interrupted the essential flow of animal spirits.

Near the last of Willis's life in the 1660s, a versatile English scientist, Robert Hooke, helped develop the compound microscope (made with more than one lens) and this instrument, though far from perfect, provided a better look at the structure of nerves. In the next decade or two microscopists began to see things in nerves that made scientists question the ancient theory of animal spirits.

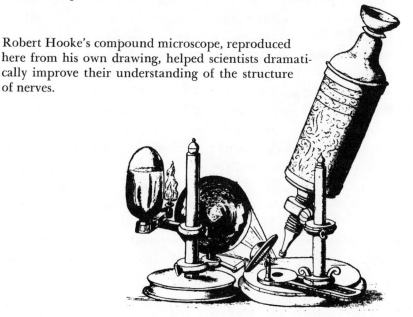

Robert Hooke's compound microscope, reproduced here from his own drawing, helped scientists dramatically improve their understanding of the structure of nerves.

For example, in Italy around 1680 Alfonso Borelli inspected the relatively large nerves running down human limbs and decided that while they might appear to be empty tubes, they were actually filled with a moist, spongy substance. As time went on, however, it looked as if as many descriptions of nerves might develop as there were microscopists looking at them. The compound microscope was a major advance for histologists (scientists who study plant and animal tissue), but the distortions were still tremendous and remained so. In 1722 the famous Dutch biologist and microscopist Anton van Leeuwenhoek saw nerve fibers as a line of globules, something like a string of beads. In 1761 a German microscopist, Martin F. Ledermüller, decided that nerve fibers were bundles of empty tubes, as many as three dozen, packed together in parallel. And as late as 1781 an Italian physician and professor of physics, Felice Fontana, decided that nerve fibers were tubes filled with a gelatinous substance.

Meanwhile, back in the late 1600s, a doubting Englishman at Cambridge University, Francis Glisson, conducted an experiment which he said disproved the existence of animal spirits. Glisson's subject was a "strong brawny man" who inserted his entire arm into a large, glass container, like a huge drinking glass. The top end was sealed so as to be watertight around the man's shoulder, except that a funnel with a small tube was inserted through the seal. Glisson used it to fill the container with water until the level of the liquid was up in the funnel itself. The brawny subject was instructed to first contract and then relax all his arm muscles, as Glisson observed the water level in the funnel. He reasoned that if animal spirits entered the arm to contract the muscles, the limb would become larger, displace the water, and cause it to rise in the funnel. But the opposite happened. As the muscles contracted, the water level dropped, and as they relaxed, the water rose. Glisson concluded that something other than animal spirits caused the contractions. He proposed that it was some form of "irritability." Although vague

10

and meaningless, the concept was still being talked about more than a century later.

In these years of the seventeenth and early eighteenth centuries many famous people came up with nerve theories. One was outlined in 1664 by a well-known English scientist, William Croone, who said that nerves carried a "rich and spiritous juice." When the mind willed that a muscle should act, Croone concluded, droplets of the juice were ejected by the appropriate nerves into the muscle. The mixture of the juice and blood caused fermentation which, in turn, made the muscular tissue swell up, forcing it into action.

Even Isaac Newton, the greatest scientist of that day and one of the greatest of all time, had his idea about the control of muscular action, although he was not a physiologist. In the second editions of two of Newton's most memorable books he proposed that the nerve force was an ether in which vibrations were set up by willpower. Newton's reputation led many to accept that he had found the definitive answer. One of Newton's admirers claimed that while the nerve ether was invisible to man it might be visible to cats and owls. Neither he nor Newton could back their assumptions with scientific evidence.

At the time, which was around 1713, interest in electricity was growing fast, and it was becoming an explanation for many natural phenomena. Some scientists decided it was responsible for life in plants and animals. They felt it was proven by the crackle of cats' fur when rubbed and by the way a human body, free of the ground, could hold an electric charge—as demonstrated by the experiment with the lad suspended on ropes. Now scientists talked about "animal electricity." Some explained that an "electric fluid" conducted animal spirits over the nerves from the brain to muscles.

Two pieces of electrical equipment became involved in eighteenth-century experiments related to nerves and muscles. One was a generator of static electricity, a hand-cranked

11

"electric influence machine." The first machine had been made in the previous century with a sulphur globe on an iron axle. It was rotated by one hand of the operator while his other hand rubbed the globe until it was electrified. The second device was the Leyden jar which could store static electricity. It was simply a jar covered with two separate coats of tinfoil, one inside and one outside the glass. The inside tinfoil was connected to an upright metal rod with a ball at the top. It stuck up out of the jar. The rod and inner foil could hold a charge of static electricity induced by an influence machine. Thus a charge could be stored in a Leyden jar for discharge when desired.

A shock from either device had surprising effects on living organisms. Applied to an animal, the electricity caused a violent contraction of its skeletal muscles. A shock delivered to a human being increased his pulse rate and glandular activity. It seemed like good medicine, and doctors administered shocks to patients. The electricity, the physicians said, stirred up and released animal spirits.

Such practices indicated that the electricity might be related to the natural power of muscular action, but this said little about the power of nerves. Did living things have their own electricity? Influence machines and Leyden jars couldn't provide the answer. It would eventually come from electrical measuring devices that didn't even exist at that time.

However, there was one interesting line of research that eventually led some people to believe that living organisms might have their own supply of electricity. For centuries Europeans had respected the torpedo, a fish that could deliver a most unpleasant sensation to anyone who touched it. The sensation had been suffered by many barefoot walkers on the beaches where torpedoes embedded themselves in the wet sand at the water's edge.

By the 1600s there were several explanations for the fish's mysterious force. One came from Florence, Italy, where a

12

scientist had dissected a torpedo and decided it was capable of shooting little "corpuscles" into its victim. Another investigator concluded that the torpedo's muscles delivered sharp blows to whatever they touched. And a third decided that the fish dealt with the same power as lightning. He was on the right track, although he could not equate the sensation with electricity because lightning had yet to be identified as electricity.

In the seventeenth and eighteenth centuries another such fish was discovered by Dutch settlers in South America. They named it the "tremblefish," though it eventually became known as the electric eel. Some of the settlers decided that the fish's sensation felt like the electric shock delivered by the recently invented Leyden jar.

In the summer of 1772 John Walsh, a member of England's House of Parliament, conducted an experiment on the Île de Ré off the coast of France where torpedoes were plentiful. He

An electric fish seen from above and in cross section, showing electric organs (a) from which electric discharge travels upward (b).

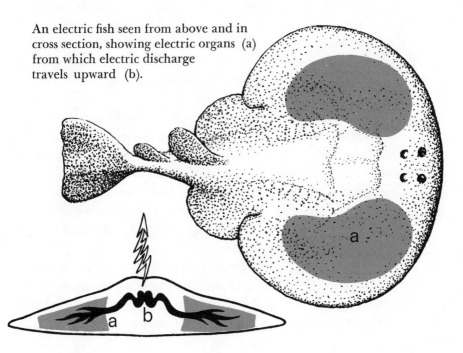

arranged five basins of water on a long table and asked four people to immerse their hands in the water so that each person's arms and body made a connection between two basins. Walsh wired the two outer basins to a live torpedo on a wet towel nearby. When the wire contacted the fish, all four human subjects felt the well-known sensation. Everyone was convinced that they had received an electric shock. They noted that when the shock came, the fish's eyes were momentarily depressed. They assumed that this showed the creature was exerting his will to send out the electricity.

In another experiment Walsh connected two wires from a fish to each side of a narrow gap made by two pieces of tinfoil. He expected to see a spark jump the gap when the fish gave his shock, but it didn't work. Some of Walsh's critics said this proved the torpedo was not electric, despite the earlier results. However, he had a scientist friend, John Hunter, do some anatomical studies on the torpedo, and the results clearly indicated that parts of the fish delivering the shock were connected with the creature's nervous system. Walsh also reviewed his experiment with the tinfoil gap and proved in a dark room that the strange creature could produce a tiny blue spark comparable to the much larger ones from Leyden jars.

Around that time, his electric-fish theory received some of its best backing from a renowned English experimenter with electricity, Henry Cavendish. He took a novel approach to the problem by constructing a model torpedo of wood, glass, metal, and sheepskin, which he then charged with forty-nine Leyden jars. He tested the model by comparing it with the real fish. For example, when he embedded the charged model in the sand on a beach and pressed his hand to the spot, the scientist felt a sensation that would come from a torpedo. ". . .There seems nothing in the phenomenon of the torpedo at all incompatible with electricity," Cavendish concluded.

By the closing decades of the eighteenth century many

14

scientists were ready to believe that Galen's animal spirits were powered the same as lightning, which had now been identified as electricity. At this time an Italian professor of anatomy was conducting the experiments with animals and electricity that were to lead to two of the most famous discoveries in all science. He was Luigi Galvani, who lived and worked in the north of Italy in the city of his birth, Bologna. He was a professor of anatomy at the University of Bologna, where he had engaged in a wide variety of laboratory investigations. They ranged from a study of ear functions to the effects of drugs on a frog's nervous system. He carefully recorded his work, but an unusual personality trait kept Galvani from publishing his findings. He was shy, but more than that, he felt that publicly describing his work could bring undue criticism and condemnation. So many of Galvani's papers remained unpublished until a half-century after his death.

His laboratory records, which were preserved among Bologna's most valuable historical treasures, indicate that his work included a study of animal electricity as early as 1771. He used a hand-operated electric influence machine to experiment with frogs' legs, which, others had found, would contract when charged by the machine. The reason was a mystery. Galvani found that the discharge could even travel over a wire from one room to another and cause the contractions in a frog's leg.

Later he became interested in the findings of Benjamin Franklin in America and Thomas François Dalibard in France, both of whom had proven that lightning was electricity (Franklin with his kite and Dalibard with a 40-foot rod). Galvani decided that the sky could be an electrical source for his frog experiments—despite the fact that lightning had killed men who had tried to repeat Franklin's kite experiment. In November 1780 he strung a wire, like a modern radio antenna, over his roof and connected it by another wire to the laboratory below. As a thunderstorm came over Bologna and lightning flashed across

15

Galvani's laboratory was pictured as above in his most famous book. His electric influence machine is shown on the left edge of the table, and his Leyden jar is on the right edge.

the sky, Galvani's frog muscles contracted when touched by the lead-in wire. In fact, Galvani soon found that only a dark cloud over the city could provide enough electrical charge to perform experiments. He, like Franklin and Dalibard, was a lucky man. A direct lightning strike might have incinerated the frogs, Galvani, and his laboratory.

This interest in atmospheric electricity led Galvani to an accidental discovery that was a major event in the long effort to unlock the mystery of nerves. One evening in September 1786, the Italian scientist suspended some freshly killed frogs on an iron railing beside the garden outside his house in Bologna. The frogs were hung on the railing by small metal hooks that pierced the spinal cords. Galvani had already found that during electrical storms he could watch the suspended frogs twitch as atmospheric electricity caused the muscles to contract. But this time, as Galvani hooked each frog into place on the railing, he was surprised by what happened.

"If the hook touched the iron railing," Galvani reported in his laboratory notes, "behold, there were spontaneous single contractions in the frogs, quite frequently. If one used a finger to push the hook against the surface of the iron, the quiescent muscles were excited as often as a push was given."

As far as he could tell, the frogs' movements were unrelated to atmospheric electricity. To make sure, he returned to his laboratory with the frog-hook preparations and laid them on an iron plate. ". . .behold, the same contractions and movements occurred as before," Galvani wrote.

He then tried the same experiment, but with a different arrangement in place of the hooks and the plate. He made small arcs of two pieces of bent metal rod joined in the center of the curve. By touching one end to a frog's spinal cord and the other to the body he could prompt muscular contractions. Soon he noticed that the response depended on something about the arcs. If the two pieces of an arc were made of the same metal, the muscular contractions were either very small or nonexistent. But if the two metals were different, the reaction was comparatively large. If the materials were non-conductors of electricity, like bone, the frog muscles did not respond at all.

A more thorough analysis of these results might have kept Galvani from jumping to a highly controversial conclusion that led to a public debate that he obviously despised. He concluded that he had finally proven the presence of animal electricity in a living organism. He reasoned that his hooks and arcs served as an avenue over which the animals' internal electricity could escape. As it flowed out through the metal, he decided, it made the frogs' muscles contract, the same as would electricity applied to the animal externally.

In 1791 the Italian professor published his ideas in a famous

17

book *De Viribus electricitatis in motu musculari commentarius* (Commentary on the Effects of Electricity on Muscular Motion). One of the most interested readers was a famous Italian physicist, Alessandro Volta, who wrote of Galvani's *Commentary* as follows:

"The treatise which appeared a few months ago concerning the action of electricity on the movement of muscles, written by Signor A. Galvani, . . . contains one of those great and brilliant discoveries which deserves to mark a new era in the annals of physics and medicine."

As Volta penned these words, he believed that Galvani's experiments were "well ordered" and that they had finally proven the presence of an inherent electricity in "all animals with either cold or warm blood." But then doubts came to the physicist's mind, and before long he claimed that the Bologna professor had not proven the presence of an internal animal electricity. Henceforth Volta refused to use the term, animal electricity. Galvani was stunned by the attack.

As it turned out, two earlier experiments similar to Galvani's had indicated that the contact of different metals might produce electricity that could influence the nerve force. One, perhaps both, of the experiments came to Volta's attention, and after some tests of his own he was convinced that the joining of dissimilar metals was a source of electricity. This conclusion also convinced him that Galvani had seriously misjudged his frog experiments. The muscular contractions, decided Volta, had resulted from electricity produced by the contact of the metals, the hooks, and the iron railing in the original instance. It was not a demonstration of an inherent animal electricity, the physicist concluded.

From 1793 to 1800 Volta published many papers and letters that supported his theory of "bimetallic electricity" and pointedly ignored animal electricity. He vigorously argued that electricity could be produced by bringing together two different metals with a third substance capable of conducting the resulting

18

flow of current. The third substance, he contended, could certainly be a frog. That being the case, the flow of electricity in the animal's muscles could cause them to contract. Galvani's conclusion was wrong, the eminent physicist declared in repeated attacks on his fellow countryman.

The attacks were not answered directly by Galvani, possibly because of his shyness and distaste for public controversy. However, they were answered by several defenders of the silent man in Bologna. The most vigorous rebuttals came from Galvani's nephew, Giovanni Aldini. But the most important document to support Galvani's discovery of an intrinsic animal electricity appeared without a signature in 1794. The anonymous paper, followed soon by an authorless supplement, was probably Galvani's work, or a joint effort with the nephew.

The unidentified experimenter said that he had surgically exposed the muscle of a frog and then touched the open area with the end of the animal's spinal cord which had been cut loose. The muscle contracted. The mystery author claimed this and a similar experiment had proven that the animal's nervous system contained enough electricity to produce a contraction. Proof or not, Volta wouldn't accept it.

But what was the truth? Actually, the two men were both right and wrong.

Galvani was right in saying that his frogs had an indwelling supply of electricity, but he was wrong in claiming that his metal hooks had released it. In the experiment without metals, assuming it was Galvani's, inherent electricity did cause the muscular contractions. The electricity in this case was later identified as the "current of injury." It becomes active when a nerve or muscle is damaged.

Volta was right in saying that the original results reported in Galvani's *Commentary* had been generated by the contact of dissimilar metals. However, he was wrong in his steadfast denial of animal electricity.

19

Out of the debate, which continued for the large part of a decade, came two great contributions to science, one from each of the principals:

From Volta came one of the greatest inventions of all time, the electric battery. It made him one of Europe's most honored scientists. The most permanent honor of all came when his name was given to the unit of electromotive force, the volt.

Galvani's contribution was less evident while he lived. He did not enjoy high honors, but died embittered in 1798. Some authorities argued that it was he who really discovered the battery, even though he failed to interpret it as such. However, little question remains as to his greatest contribution. He convinced many scientists that the nerve force was electricity, and he thereby opened up a new view of the nervous system through the science of electrophysiology (the study of natural electrical functions of living plants and animals. Galvani's work marked the end of centuries and centuries of Galen's animal spirits, and it brought men much closer to understanding the great mysteries of life and thought.

Due honor was given to the professor of Bologna after his death. The electricity of the battery that he had prompted Volta to invent became known as *galvanic*. Today, in fact, Webster's New International Dictionary gives nearly four dozen words or variations of words derived from Galvani's name. One of the most important is *galvanometer*, the device for detecting and measuring small electric currents. The instrument eventually became the key to unlock the final, scientific proof about the nerve force.

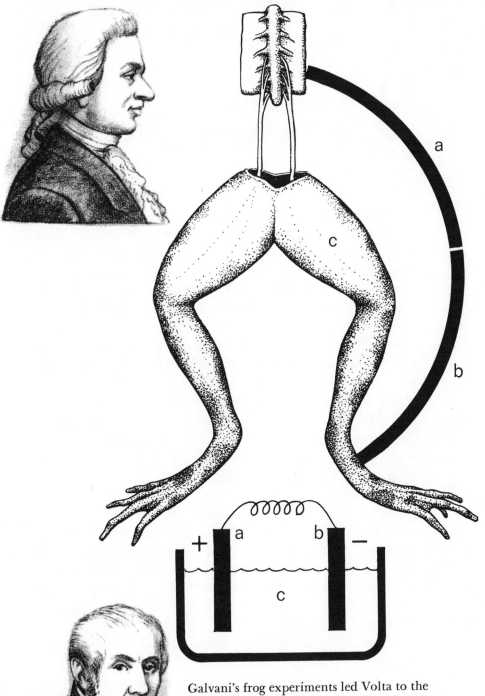

Galvani's frog experiments led Volta to the invention of the battery, which also depended upon different metals (a and b) with a third substance (c) capable of conducting electric current.

3 The Remarkable Nerve Galvanometer

Discoveries in the nervous system have usually had to wait for discoveries or improvements in technology. One such waiting period occurred in the half-century after Galvani's death. At best, his evidence of an inherent animal electricity was empirical and based on limited facts. Direct, unquestionable evidence had to come from an instrument that could detect small amounts of current.

Until the 1800s electricity was usually detected in two ways: by seeing a spark jump a gap or by feeling a shock (this included observing the contraction of a muscle when it was shocked). But sparks and shocks, except with powerful electric fish, could hardly serve as indicators for the minute amounts of electricity in the nervous system. This required something entirely new, an extremely sensitive instrument for detecting and measuring electricity.

The galvanometer invented in 1820 was the right instrument, but early models were usually too insensitive to detect nerve electricity. Or when a sensitive enough instrument was developed, the attempt to detect nerve electricity was confused by small, extraneous amounts of current created when the metal electrodes contacted the living tissue. So the final proof that nerves were electrical required both a highly sensitive instrument and special kinds of electrodes.

Both problems were solved around 1850 by a brilliant young scientist in Germany, Emil Du Bois-Reymond, a student of one of the nineteenth century's most famous physiologists, Johannes Müller. Du Bois-Reymond developed a set of "nonpolarizable" electrodes, and he proved that they wouldn't generate currents of their own to deceive the experimenter. Then he designed a remarkable galvanometer. All the moving parts were extremely light. The coils were wound of the purest, finest copper wire obtainable. The purity meant that it was comparatively free from bits of iron that might adversely influence the magnetic needle. The fineness of the wire enabled Du Bois-Reymond to make three times more windings than found in the best galvanometers. When complete, the instrument was undoubtedly the most sensitive in the world. Du Bois-Reymond called it a *nerve galvanometer.*

Actually the instrument, when first applied to a nerve, gave no indication of electricity, but the scientist soon found a way of obtaining a reading. He made a tiny cut or injury on the nerve at a point along its extremity. He placed one galvanometer electrode on the injured place and the other on an intact section of the nerve. Then electricity suddenly flowed through the instrument. Du Bois-Reymond had, like Galvani, also encountered the phenomenon that would become known years later as the *current of injury.* Regardless, the German had truly detected nerve electricity. He had accomplished what had evaded so many other scientists for so long.

Soon Du Bois-Reymond made another important discovery. He found that various kinds of stimulation at one point on a nerve caused a momentary change in the electricity being picked up from another point on the same nerve. The stimulus might be mechanical, a slight tap, or it might be electrical, a small shock. When the stimulus was applied, Du Bois-Reymond's galvanometer responded in a way that was difficult to explain. The needle showing the steady value of the current of injury suddenly turned and pointed in the opposite direction, revealing that the electricity had reversed direction. But the reversal was only momentary, and the needle swung back, indicating that the electrical flow had now returned to its original direction.

23

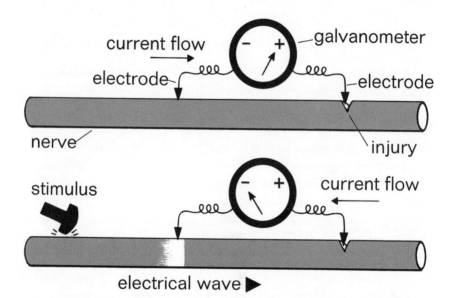

current flow

galvanometer

electrode

electrode

nerve

injury

stimulus

current flow

electrical wave ▶

Du Bois-Reymond's discovery: When galvanometer electrodes were touched to intact and injured points on a nerve, electric current flowed left to right (top). When the nerve was stimulated the current momentarily reversed flow (bottom), indicating passage of nerve impulse.

Actually the change on the galvanometer was an indication of an electrical wave that moved along the nerve after being set off by the stimulus.

Du Bois-Reymond referred to this electrical activity as *negative variation* because he recognized that an electrically positive point on a stimulated nerve briefly turned negative. It was several years before this phenomenon was even partly understood. It then became evident that there was not a constant flow of electricity in an uninjured nerve, only a capability of electrical activity. The break in an injured nerve, in a sense, activated the capability and current flowed. But more important, stimulation of an uninjured nerve could also release the electrical capability, and the result was a wave of activity that raced along the nerve.

24

This was the nerve impulse. In finding it Du Bois-Reymond had finally identified the nerve force. Now he had really unmasked the "spirit" of "animal spirits."

However, the German scientist had no more pinned down the fact that nerves were definitely electrical when another great scientist completed an intricate experiment in 1850 and seemed to confuse the whole picture. It had to do with the speed of nerve messages.

By this time people were aware that electricity moved extremely fast. Samuel Morse's invention of the telegraph in the 1840s certainly revealed it. And the telegraph and nervous system were definitely open to comparison. In the living organism lines of nerves spread out from the brain and spinal cord like telegraph lines, and they clearly carried messages to and from various parts of the body. Exactly how fast was a question because the speed of electricity had yet to be measured, but the telegraph indicated that the velocity was tremendous. A New York telegrapher could tap his key and receive a response in the blink of an eye from a Washington operator, nearly two hundred miles away. But then the experiment of 1850 proved otherwise.

It was conducted by Hermann von Helmholtz, a physiologist and physicist, who had also studied under the renowned Johannes Müller. Helmholtz's test was one that Müller had believed virtually impossible. In 1833 he had written that "we shall probably never attain the power of measuring the velocity of nervous action." He thought it was too fast to measure over the short distances in a living nervous system. The speeds had been estimated at various velocities, from 9,000 feet a minute to 57,600,000,000 feet a second.

Helmholtz solved the problem with an intricate device that revealed the speed of nervous action in the frog was only 82 to 130 feet per second, less than 90 miles per hour. At this rate a message over the New York-to-Washington telegraph line would have taken more than two hours one way.

Why was electricity so fast in wire but slow in nerves? This was unanswerable at the time. The secret was locked into the fine, microscopic structure of nerves, and no instrument was powerful enough to unravel the answer. It had to wait for improved microscopes and other technical advances of the future.

Meanwhile scientists continued exploring the electrical phenomena of the nervous system, and they turned up some historic results. The work was especially remarkable because the keys to understanding what happened remained in the galvanometer and galvanic battery, unbelievably primitive equipment for dealing with the tiny, complicated electrical events of the nervous system. As was learned later, the early pioneers of the science were working with the thousandth part of a volt. It's a wonder of science that any results were obtained at all.

Two of the most important accomplishments are now known by the initials ESB and EEG. The first stands for electrical stimulation of the brain, the second for electroencephalogram, better known as brain waves.

In April 1870 two physicians in Berlin, Germany, Gustav Fritsch and Eduard Hitzig, completed a report of some unusual experiments. The work had apparently been prompted when Hitzig served as the head physician in a military hospital where in certain cases the brains of patients had been exposed by gunshot wounds that had torn holes in their skulls. The report told of how he had used a galvanic battery to stimulate the exposed human brain (which has no sense of pain itself) with tiny electric shocks. Hitzig observed that whenever the electricity was applied to points near the back of the brain, it made a patient's eyes move.

The ghoulish results prompted Hitzig and Fritsch to try similar experiments on animals. The two men, according to one report, had no laboratory, so the work was carried out in Hitzig's home on Frau (Mrs.) Hitzig's dressing table. Here they stimu-

26

Electrically stimulating certain points (a, b, c, d) on exposed brains of dogs, Fritsch and Hitzig noted muscular responses in the animals (a, b, c, d).

lated the brains of live dogs with galvanic currents after surgically cutting holes through the skulls while the animals were under anesthesia. They soon recognized that some areas of the brain were motor, and related to the control of muscular movement, but other areas were not. When weak currents were applied with electrodes to the motor areas, certain muscles of the body contracted in response to the stimulation, and as the electrodes were moved around the exposed brains, different muscles responded. From such tests upon a number of dogs Fritsch and Hitzig recognized that all brains were generally alike as to what area controlled what bodily muscles.

Thus two German doctors gave scientists one of their most valuable methods for mapping the brain locations of its different functional regions. Not long before this time the brain was

27

thought of as sort of a magic black box with all parts related to all of the organ's functions. Then scientists slowly began to recognize that different brain areas served different purposes. Animal experiments, for example, showed that certain bodily functions could be destroyed by surgically removing parts of a living creature's brain. Also, diseases and head injuries that destroyed certain areas of human brains provided similar evidence. One of the most famous cases was reported from Cavendish, Vermont, where an accidental blast hurled an iron rod through the head of a railroad construction foreman, Phineas Gage. He lived for twelve years with part of his brain torn away, but his personality was markedly changed by the accident. He became undependable as a workman and wandered aimlessly from job to job. And his language was marked by an unusual amount of cursing. Fritsch and Hitzig's ESB offered a less destructive, more scientific means of learning about detailed functions of the brain.

ESB was soon used on humans. In 1874 an American doctor at Cincinnati, Ohio, reported that he had applied electrical stimulation to the brain of a young woman, who had a hole in her skull as the result of cancer. The doctor took advantage of the unusual opening to insert needle electrodes into the woman's brain. When a battery was connected to the electrodes, it caused the patient's leg, arm, and neck muscles to contract. Her limbs moved dramatically, and her head suddenly deflected. Such experiments on humans were few and far apart until this century when brain surgery became relatively common. Then ESB was used to great advantage in mapping human brains to show surgeons what functions might be impaired by removal of different parts of the brain.

ESB was employed much earlier in animal studies. One of the most famous investigators was David Ferrier, an Englishman who began a systematic study of brain functions in the 1870s. He worked mostly on the brains of monkeys and apes mapping out much of what we now know about the motor cortex (the cortex is the brain's wrinkled outer surface of gray matter, and a large area of it is devoted to motor control of muscular movements).

As Fritsch and Hitzig introduced ESB, a relatively new instrument was being used to demonstrate the electrical properties of nerves. It was a *reflecting galvanometer* developed a dozen years earlier by the famous British mathematician and physicist, Lord William Kelvin. Electricity applied to the instrument's coils caused a small mirror to turn slightly. A light directed upon the mirror was reflected as a spot on a nearby scale. It served as the galvanometer's indicator instead of the usual needle. Even an imperceptibly small deflection of the mirror produced a relatively large movement of the spot on the scale. It worked like a hand-held mirror reflecting the sun on a wall. A slight wiggle of the mirror causes a big movement of the distant spot. In the galvanometer this acted as a kind of optical magnification, greatly increasing the instrument's sensitivity.

The new device was excellent for demonstrating the electrical activity of nerves. It was especially good for classroom use because an entire student body could watch the results displayed on the scale. It was thus used in the early 1870s by an English teacher of physiology, Richard Caton, who gave his classes demonstrations of Du Bois-Reymond's negative variation. The new instrument led Caton to a fabulous discovery of his own.

It apparently began when the Englishman became interested in Fritsch and Hitzig's demonstration of how electrical activity flowing out from the brain to motor nerves caused muscular action. Caton wondered if the same phenomena might occur with the incoming sensory nerves. Did they direct electricity inward from sensory organs (eyes, ears, taste buds, etc.) to the brain? If so, would it be possible to detect this electrical activity at the brain's surface? Caton decided to find out.

For the research he obtained a grant from the British Medical Association and went to work on monkeys and rabbits.

29

With the animals anesthetized he surgically opened their skulls to expose the brains. When he touched his galvanometer electrodes to the wrinkled layers of gray matter, the reflected action on the scale was surprising. The little light kept moving back and forth, indicating that an endless flow of changing electrical potentials (voltages) were being picked up by the electrodes. Close observation showed that the resulting currents flowing through the galvanometer were continually changing directions. They didn't appear to be messages from incoming sensory nerves, for the steady electrical oscillations occurred without any apparent sensory impressions. They were obviously an indication that the living brain is a source of on-going electrical activity.

As he continued experimenting on different animals, Caton did find signs of sensory messages. They showed up as variations in the constant flow of changing electricity. In one instance his electrodes were on an area of a rabbit's brain that David Ferrier had related to the muscular control of chewing. When food was only shown to the animal, it caused an electrical variation in the brain.

In one of the most interesting experiments Caton recognized that electrical changes in the brain were prompted by a light directed into the eyes of monkeys and rabbits. When he shaded

In 1875 mysterious electrical brain waves were discovered by Richard Caton, who also associated them with variations in light

left side

eye opening

right side

the light from the animal's eyes, the electrical effect on the brain was diminished. It is interesting to note that the light source was described by Caton as a "flame" (perhaps a candle or gaslight). The recently invented electric lightbulb was not yet used in his laboratory.

With these fascinating results, Caton apparently paid little attention to what may have been his most important discovery: that the brain's feeble currents could even be picked up from the surface of an animal's skull. This was really the discovery of the *electroencephalogram* (EEG) as we now think of it. It was one of the most important findings in the history of the science of the brain.

The full story of this remarkable discovery has some interesting sequels. Caton publicly presented the report of the experiments to his supporting organization, the British Medical Association; therefore, the record of his findings appeared in 1875 in the Association's publication, the *British Medical Journal*. This meant that Caton's classic paper was read primarily by physicians and not by scientists who would have had the greatest interest in the report. For them to see the material it should have appeared in a scientific journal covering physiology. As a result, brain waves were "discovered" again—not once but several times.

entering the eye. A modern EEG shows how the pattern of brain waves changes with opening and closing of the eyes.

▼ eye closure

Fifteen years after publication of Caton's report a famous European journal of science carried a growing debate between a Polish and a Viennese scientist. Both claimed to have discovered brain waves. Caton soon settled the dispute with a letter referring to his earlier report in the *British Medical Journal*. Then it turned out that prior to this incident, but after Caton's discovery, several European scientists had also discovered brain waves. A Russian had even connected a telephone receiver to an animal's brain and listened to strange sounds set up by the EEG.

A half-century later brain waves were detected in the *human* brain. The discoverer this time was a secretive Viennese psychiatrist, Hans Berger, who had attached electrodes to his young son's scalp during experiments conducted in a secluded laboratory at the University of Jena, Germany. Berger recognized that some of the waves of electricity from his son's head oscillated about ten times per second. He kept his findings secret for five years, but then revealed them in 1929 in the first of fourteen papers published on the EEG over the next decade.

As these papers reported, Berger intensively pursued the study of brain waves and laid out much of the basic knowledge and techniques for electroencephalography, which would be used to study the brain for various purposes. He recognized that the comparatively large, 10-per-second waves were the predominant waves among a number of lesser electrical oscillations with different frequencies. He named the large ones *alpha waves* and assigned other letters of the Greek alphabet to the lesser waves.

Berger noticed that alpha waves seemed to flow relatively undisturbed when his human subjects were relaxed physically and mentally. When this state of consciousness was disturbed, so were the alpha waves. The sound of a pistol shot would cause them to disappear leaving only the lesser waves. Even the prick of a finger with a pin would cause them to change. The psychiatrist found that sleep affected the subject's brain waves, and certain drugs caused them to disappear, as they put the subject to sleep.

Then Berger proposed that these electrical wave patterns issuing from the human head could be useful in diagnosing abnormal conditions of the brain caused by disease or physical damage. The problems would be revealed in abnormal patterns of brain waves. This was borne out in his study of a dozen patients suffering from epilepsy caused by a disorder of the brain.

At first scientists generally ignored Berger's work, but then two English scientists, one a Nobel Prize winner, proved the validity of the Austrian's reports, and henceforth many outstanding scientists and doctors investigated brain waves. As they proceeded, using better and better electronic recording equipment, they learned a great deal about the intricate electrical patterns that can be recorded from the human scalp. Primarily the EEG soon became a major medical tool for assisting neurologists in diagnosing brain damage.

Thousands and thousands of miles of the long wriggly lines of human brain waves have been recorded and studied, but even today scientists can't explain for sure what causes these endless flows of electrical activity that Hans Berger first discovered on his son's head.

As all these discoveries of the nineteenth and early twentieth centuries were revealed, they proved that the brain, spinal cord, and nerves were complicated, baffling electrical systems. But as the picture evolved during the last century, even the most knowledgeable scientist could only guess as to the electrical origins of this marvelous, mysterious force of life. If some kind of a natural battery was involved it was surely the smallest in the universe. Some surmised that the electrical source of the nervous system was to be found in the fascinating nerve cell, whose infinitesimally small structures had been the subject of serious microscopic studies since the 1830s.

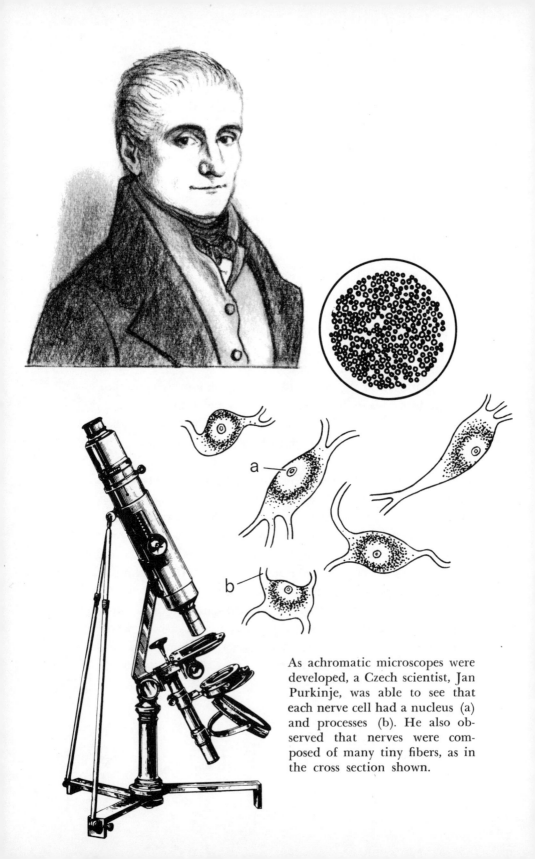

As achromatic microscopes were developed, a Czech scientist, Jan Purkinje, was able to see that each nerve cell had a nucleus (a) and processes (b). He also observed that nerves were composed of many tiny fibers, as in the cross section shown.

4 Form and Function

Uɴᴛɪʟ ᴛʜᴇ 1830s progress in microscopy was held back by *chromatic aberration,* which meant that lenses produced a rainbow effect on the fringes of enlarged images so as to distort them. The more scientists tried to magnify something, the more serious the distortions became. Many authorities decided that the power of microscopes would always be limited by chromatic aberration. The same was true for the telescope until the late 1700s when an English optician, John Dollond, combined two different kinds of glass in lenses and overcame the color distortion. Dollond's idea eventually led to an achromatic (free from color) microscope, and the new, more powerful instrument became widely available in the 1830s.

One was obtained in 1832 by Jan Evangelista Purkinje, a Czechoslovakian who held the chair of physiology at the University of Breslau, Germany. Purkinje was a man of many interests. He had already studied vision and color, and he had tried to figure out why a person becomes dizzy when the body is rotated. His new achromatic microscope was received with great excitement. He reported that he and his students focused the instrument upon animal tissue "with real wolf's hunger."

Five years later Purkinje made a historic presentation in Prague at a Congress of natural scientists and physicians. He told of studies conducted on tissue drawn from the central nervous systems of animals. The Czech scientist had been able to see nerve cells well enough to describe them accurately for the first time. He had made drawings from the observations and they showed that each nerve cell seen in brains and spinal cords had a *nucleus* (a small central kernel in a main body) with *processes* (fibers extending outward from the body). Purkinje's descriptions of certain brain cells were so accurate that they eventually became identified by his name. The physiologist had also made another important observation concerning the threadlike nerves that run through the body. He could see that they were formed from bundles of many, many very fine fibers.

Purkinje's contributions to the science of nerves and brain were especially remarkable when one considers the timing of his report at Prague. It was presented months before two famous German scientists worked out and published the cell theory of life, one of the most momentous ideas in the history of biology. In 1838 a botanist, Matthias Schleiden, presented a cell theory for plants, and the following year a physiologist, Theodor Schwann, clarified the idea and extended it to animals. The theory simply said that all living things consist of cells. Purkinje had already described the cell that made up the nervous system.

Still, his description of the nerve cell was barely a start in the long search for an understanding of how the brain, spinal cord, and nerves work. The Czech physiologist was unable to explain why the cell body had fibers extending from it, or how

The difficulties early microscopists faced in studying a single cell among millions is illustrated by this drawing. It shows the relationship of a certain cell body to the length of its axon.

one of the cells related to the others. However, he had made a giant step forward in comprehending the function of the nervous system by learning about its structure.

Soon Hermann von Helmholtz, the scientist who later measured the speed of the nerve impulse, took up the microscopic study of the threadlike nerves running through living organisms, and he agreed with Purkinje that they consisted of fibers all bundled together. He proposed that these fibers were actually the extremely fine extension of nerve cells, but he couldn't prove it.

Then a revealing observation came from Johannes Müller's laboratory. It was made by a young student from Denmark, A. H. Hannover, as he competed for a prize offered by the Royal Society of Science of Denmark to the person who could best use the microscope to understand the nervous system. Hannover studied the processes of nerve cells and recognized that some of them were much longer than anyone had thought. His observation supported Helmholtz's idea that the fine, barely visible fibers making up nerves were acutally bundles of the processes of nerve cells.

As better microscopes revealed more about the nerve cell's form, they still offered little evidence of how one cell related to another. Understanding the relationship could be an important key to unlocking the secrets of the nervous system. It might help scientists determine how the tiny basic parts of the system worked together to carry their electrical "messages" between the brain and all parts of the body. And it might be especially important in figuring out the circuits for the electrical activity of the nervous system.

The problem of relationships, however, confronted the histologist with one of his most difficult tests. It was hard enough to observe nerve cells as a whole, but this work required the clear viewing of only parts of single cells in the areas where they came together with other cells. It was a bewildering challenge, for it required looking into an unimaginably complex thicket of cell

37

bodies and fibers to decide on what processes belonged to what cells and how they were connected, if connected at all.

This kind of exploration not only called for powerful microscopes, but it required new methods of preparing tissue from nerves, spinal cords, and brains so the cells would visibly stand out in contrast to one another. The search for the desired microscopic preparation was in the hands of Europe's top histologists, and it took much of the last half of the nineteenth century. Their specific interest was known as *neurohistology*. Their problems were threefold.

First came the matter of "fixing" the living characteristics of nerve tissue so it appeared as lifelike as possible after being pressed into a thin microscope slide. It was largely a matter of trying to find the best chemicals for quickly preserving the features of living nerve tissue as it was dying (and changing rapidly) in the preparation of slides. Advances were made in this area, and fairly soon the problem had become relatively minor.

Second, neurohistologists had to find a way of "sectioning" tissue into ultra-thin, transparent slices so the viewer could see through the material. But it was more than a matter of making the slices transparent. The thinner a section of tissue, the fewer the nerve cells the microscopist was forced to look at under his lenses. In effect, he was cutting away all but a comparatively few of the thousands and thousands of cells in even the smallest sample of tissue. His observations were thereby less confusing. This problem was largely solved by the development of the *microtome* around the middle of the nineteenth century. The microtome was an extremely thin, sharp knife in a guide, like a small guillotine, which sliced down through tissue held firmly on the base. The device could cut a thinner, evener section than had been possible with a hand-held knife. Purkinje used one of the first microtomes.

The third was the most trying of the neurohistologist's problems, but it held the greatest possibilities for the persistent,

38

patient investigator. When nerve tissue was viewed through the microscope, the visual contrast between the cells or parts of cells was so poor that the dividing lines were fuzzy, and everything blended together. This distorted the view of small but important details of cells, even when the tissue had been well fixed and carefully sectioned. The answer was to be found by staining some parts of the tissues to increase the contrast and make the outlines of cells stand out visually. The search for effective stains became the longest and most important part of the effort to unveil the elusive secrets of nerve cell structure.

In the 1850s a German histologist, Joseph von Gerlach, came upon an excellent stain for nerve tissue. It was a rich pigment, carmine, made from the dried bodies of female cochineal insects. Oddly, carmine had already served as a stain in microscopy. Three quarters of a century earlier it had been applied to wood to improve the contrast of fibers for better viewing under the microscope. Unaware that it would work on nerve, Gerlach accidentally left some tissue in a carmine solution overnight and found the visual contrast immensely improved. He observed nerve cells as they had never been seen before.

The carmine stain advanced the understanding of the cell's structure considerably. It now became pretty clear that among the many processes branching out from each cell body there was one dominant fiber, which became known as the *axon*. This led to wide agreement that bundles of these tiny axons formed the hairlike nerves which run through the bodies of animals and humans.

The improved staining method still didn't provide the evidence that could settle basic questions about the relationships between cells; however, it had a lot to do with the advancement of two theories on the subject. Soon they were the subject of heated debate.

On one side were the "reticularists." Their theory came from Gerlach who proposed that nerve cells were all connected,

39

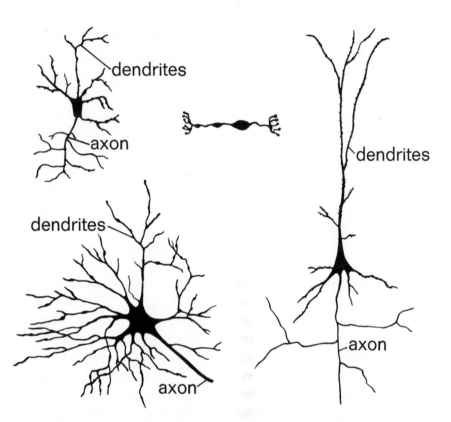

In the last century the Golgi preparation, a new staining process for nerve tissue, allowed microscopists to see the outlines of cells (as reproduced above) more clearly than ever.

making the nervous system one great, unbroken reticulum, or network, of cell bodies and fibers. This was the *reticulum theory* (network theory). Neurohistologists who rejected the network idea became the "anti-reticularists." For a long time little evidence was available to support their negative position.

The reticulum theory's greatest strength eventually came from an Italian anatomist and physician, Camillo Golgi, after he had developed a remarkable new stain around 1873. His staining process was complicated. Tissue had to be treated in several steps for several days in various chemical solutions before it was ready to be mounted and viewed. The Golgi stain made cells of all kinds stand out like etchings in silver and black. It enabled the Italian scientist to pick out details in cells never recognized before. The minute structures that Golgi discovered are still identified with his name.

When applied to nerve tissue, the new stain revealed details of the bodies and processes of cells better than ever. Not only could Golgi see the large main fiber, the axon, of each cell but he had a clearer view of the many smaller branchings, which became known as *dendrites*. However, the stain was still not good enough to enable its founder to say for sure how one cell related to another. But Golgi chose to support the reticulum theory, and it was a big boost for the reticularists. In fact, the Italian scientist was soon their chosen leader.

Then Golgi's career took a turn that must have disconcerted his fellow reticularists. He became thoroughly frustrated trying to figure out the nervous system. The clarity offered by his stain only made him surer than ever that the great tangled web of cells was too complex, too baffling for human understanding. So Golgi quit the field, saying it was a fruitless effort. Turning to other areas of medicine he eventually became famous for a treatment of malaria. Possibly the Italian regretted his move—especially in 1906 when he shared the Nobel Prize with Santiago Ramón y Cajal, a Spanish microscopist who had found ways of seeing nerve cells in their true forms.

Cajal was a giant of a scientist from a country that had produced hardly any scientists at all. Early in life he had fallen in love with the microscope, and he and the instrument were inseparable. Through his lenses he felt he was party to the world's most enthralling drama. The Spanish histologist was said to have once spent twenty hours in one sitting before his microscope watching a single biological event unfold.

"Come with me to the laboratory," Cajal once wrote in a popular magazine. "There upon the stage of the microscope, tear up the petal of a flower, forgetting for a moment its beauty and

41

The Spanish microscopist Ramón y Cajal dramatically advanced understanding of nerve-cell structure with new techniques. (Drawings, after Cajal, are of nerve cells from the brain of a hen.)

fragrance. Then take a bit of animal tissue; tear it apart without compunction even though it pulsates and trembles at the touch of the needle, and the leaf of the plant and the tissue of the animal will reveal to you in every part the same structure—a sort of honeycomb built up of little cells and more little cells, separated by connective substance, and harboring the honey of life in the form of semisolid, granular material, encircling a tiny corpuscle, the nucleus."

Of all cells none fascinated the Spaniard more than the nerve cell. To him it was the aristocrat of all bodily structures. Cajal felt that in the nerve cell scientists might find the physical basis of such mysterious forces as thought, will, instinct, and the association of ideas.

One time during a visit to a well-known Madrid doctor, Cajal was introduced to the Golgi stain. Back in his laboratory he applied it to nerve tissue and saw the unbelievably complex thicket of fibrous cells with great clarity. Interestingly, Cajal sensed the same frustration that drove Golgi away from the study of the nervous system, but the Spanish histologist was more tenacious, and he pursued a twofold attack to find the secrets hidden in the maze of fibers.

First Cajal refused to believe that the Golgi stain was beyond improvement. He painstakingly tried many variations on the process and applied them to nerve tissue. Eventually he made improvements that advanced the microscopic clarity of his slides. When Golgi learned of this accomplishment (well after it had happened) he was obviously irritated, and the bad feelings, which he directed against Cajal personally, lasted to the end of the Italian's days.

Second, the Spaniard attacked the problem with another technique that most scientists, including Golgi, had also abandoned as being too delicate and too complicated. It consisted of staining and studying bits of embryonic nerve tissue (meaning that the tissue was in its earliest stages of life) from birds and small mammals. By selecting samples at different points during the various creatures' earliest periods of growth Cajal was able to envisage how individual nerve cells developed and how they came together. The work required making hundreds of slides meticulously prepared with the improved Golgi stain. Slowly the persistent Spanish histologist pieced together an idea of how the cells of the fully grown nervous system related to one another.

This happened in the late 1880s when Cajal was still an obscure Spanish anatomist. Despite the importance of his findings he was unable, as hard as he might try, to catch the attention of scientists who should be interested. He even pub-

43

lished his own scientific journal, *The Trimonthly Review of Normal and Pathological Histology*. In it he printed his own papers that had been turned down by other publications. He could only afford to print sixty copies and mail them to scientists around Europe. Still no one paid attention. The recipients either didn't read the reports or looked upon them as the work of some deranged person with silly visions of attaining scientific fame. It was somewhat understandable. Here was an unknown man publishing his own work in a country with no prominent histologists, and he was claiming to have accomplished what the greatest men in the field had abandoned as impossible. It seemed preposterous.

Meanwhile the arguments between reticularists and anti-reticularists continued. The latter were joined in 1887 by two prominent European scientists, Wilhelm His and August Forel, who proposed that the branchings of nerve cells ended freely in the gray matter of the brain and spinal cord. But like others, His and Forel were unable to prove their theory because their microscopic preparations were inadequate for the job.

In 1889 Cajal, the obscure Spaniard with the answer, finally decided to take his case in person to the leading figures in anatomy as they met in Berlin for that year's meeting of the German Anatomical Society. Using all of his savings Cajal traveled to the German capital. As one of the last at the conference to give a presentation, the Spaniard amazed Europe's greatest histologists. They were abruptly awakened to the fact that a peculiar visitor from Spain had dealt the reticulum theory a devastating blow. Cajal's masterful slides had the damaging proof. The surprised onlookers recognized that they could no longer say with assurance that nerve cells were all woven together in an unbroken network. Cajal made it pretty clear that they were independent units, and thereby he offered the basis for a new theory, which was called the *neuron theory*.

But this was only the beginning of Cajal's great contributions to the neurological sciences. Returning to his laboratory he continued working on techniques to improve the microscopic view of nerve cells. Most of all he concentrated upon the improvement of staining methods which he felt were the key to success. He once wrote:

"For the biologist every advance in staining technique is like gaining a new sense with which to explore the unknown. As if Nature were determined to keep hidden from our eyes the marvelous structure of the cell, this magnificent protagonist of life is obstinately concealed in the double invisibility of smallness and homogeneity. Structures of amazing complexity appear under the microscope colorless, uniform and as simple in architecture as a mass of jelly."

Cajal drew more and more revealing details of nerve cells out of their tiny hiding places. For example, he continued his observations upon the tissue of birds and small animals and recognized a fundamental pattern common to all nerve cells. In studying cells in the visual and olfactory (smell) systems of various animal subjects, Cajal noted that axons always emerged from the cell body pointing *toward* the brain, and the dendrites grew toward the outside world, on the side of the cell away from the brain.

Realizing that sensory messages in such systems naturally flow inward, the Spanish scientist deduced that nerve impulses were conducted from dendrites to axons via the neuron bodies. He thus concluded that he had determined the direction of flow for the electrical activity of all nerve cells. This led to the further conclusion that the flow of impulses in any part of the nervous system was determined by how the cells grew into place. In other words, the electrical circuits of the brain, spinal cord, and nerves are determined by the growth patterns of nerve cells, and the circuits are connected up in the earliest stages of life through synapses (the point where the cells communicate).

The Spaniard also noted a remarkable variation in cells as he studied nerve tissue drawn from different animal species found

45

on different levels of the evolutionary scale with varying levels of intellectual power. The higher animals with greater intellects had more synaptic connections between their nerve cells than lower animals. From this observation Cajal surmised that intellectual accomplishments might actually increase the cell connections of the brain.

For his accomplishments Cajal shared the Nobel Prize of 1906 with Golgi. The Spanish scientist continued his important work for more than a quarter of a century, until his death in 1934. Golgi lived only until 1926, and to the end the Italian defended the reticulum theory. Even after his death it was promoted for many more years by a few other scientists. Textbooks continued describing the discredited theory as late as the 1940s. By then the lingering controversy was finally ended when the new electron microscopes were trained upon nerve cells right after World War II. Their great power enabled histologists to see, without question, that an ultra-narrow gap existed between practically all nerve cells at the synapse. The cells, as Cajal had stated over sixty years earlier, were definitely independent units, not just tiny lumps on an endless web of fibers.

In the late 1940s another Nobel Prize winner, the eminent English scientist Sir Charles Sherrington, summarized why the work of his friend, Cajal, was so important:

"He solved at a stroke the great question of the direction of nerve-currents in their travel through brain and spinal cord. He showed, for instance, that each nerve path is always a line of one-way traffic only, and that the direction of that traffic is at all times irreversibly the same. The so-called nerve networks [proposed by the reticulum theory] with unfixed direction of travel he swept away. The nerve-circuits are valved, he said, and he was able to point out where the valves lie—namely where one cell meets the next."

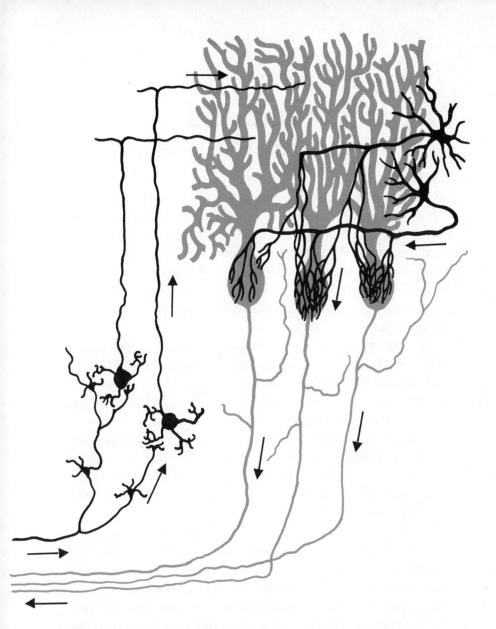

Cajal discovered that impulses move in only one direction along
nerve fibers, as indicated in this adaptation from one of his drawings of brain cells.

5 Electronic and Nerve Messages

THE NEUROLOGICAL scientists of the last century—like Du Bois-Reymond and Cajal—must be listed as the great masters in the most fundamental of all sciences: man's brain trying to understand itself. With simple, clumsy galvanometers and microscopes they made amazing discoveries that would have been major accomplishments even had they been made in this century. With their primitive tools these men were far ahead of their times.

Still, many scientific advances were unattainable for them because of their limited instruments. Further progress had to wait on twentieth-century developments. The waiting period extended into the first decades of this century. In those years advancements in the science of nerves and brain seemed to rest on a plateau along the steep, upward trail leading to an understanding of the nervous system. It was a little like the period following Galvani's discovery, when the proof of nerve electricity had to wait upon the invention and improvement of the galvanometer.

Around the 1920s the science again began to move dramatically forward. The greatest boost came from the invention of the thermionic vacuum triode, the radio tube that became the basis of electronic amplifiers so common in today's radios, televisions, and record players (where transistors are now used as well as vacuum tubes). The new tube offered the capability of amplifying, or enlarging, small electric potentials to tremendous values. For example, it made possible amplification of tiny signals caught from the atmosphere by a radio receiver. The invention led to many other astonishing developments as the age of electronics matured.

Not long after the first tube was developed, the ancient galvanometer was replaced by the sophisticated and highly sensitive cathode ray oscilloscope. Instead of appearing on a dial the oscilloscope readings were displayed in graph form on the face of an electronic tube, like the modern TV screen. Now scientists could detect the smallest imaginable voltages, magnify them immensely with an amplifier, and then observe them on a cathode ray oscilloscope. The results on the screen not only indicated the electrical values involved but also showed in curve form how the values were changing with the passage of time.

While the laymen of the 1920s were marveling at the newly invented radio, they paid little attention to scientists who were putting the amplifier tube to work in studying the nervous system. Now the elusive electricity that Du Bois-Reymond had struggled so hard to detect could be magnified to surprising proportions. Even the electrical activity of a single neuron could be analyzed.

In 1931 a famous English scientist Edgar D. Adrian pointed out in a lecture at the University of Pennsylvania that the electrical power of a single nerve axon of a frog would be in the order of .00000000000001 watt. But with the radio amplifier, he explained, this minuscule wattage could easily be magnified to 50,000 watts or more. In fact, he said, the electrical activity in a single nerve axon of a frog could be broadcasted as a signal so that millions of listeners could tune in and hear the sounds made by the cell's electricity.

The next year, in December 1932, Adrian won the Nobel Prize for Physiology or Medicine for his discoveries related to the nerve cell. He and his co-workers at Cambridge University in England used thermionic vacuum tubes to amplify the electrical activity of single nerve axons in order to study the action of individual cells. To do this they had to deal with thousandths of a volt (millivolts). Their amplified nerve voltages were transmitted to a special oscillograph, a mechanical version of the

49

cathode ray oscilloscope. It made a graphlike recording of the changing electrical activity on a strip of photographic film. This not only allowed the scientists to study curves representing the nerve electricity, but it enabled them to observe the wave form of the electrical action that occurred during the split second when a nerve impulse was conducted along an axon.

From this research the English workers discovered a most basic principle of nerve cells, the all-or-none principle. They found that the cell is either fully on or completely off electrically. It works as if the neuron were controlled by some internal switch. When the right stimulus forces the cell into action, the imaginary switch turns on for a moment, and then promptly turns off. During the "on" interval a specific amount of current flows in the cell, no more, no less.

This was a most fundamental discovery in the long struggle to learn how the nervous system works. It was basic information for further understanding the function of the massive, complicated web of cells that make up the system's amazing tissue. It was the kind of key discovery that brings Nobel Prizes.

While Adrian and his associates at Cambridge were applying their new electronic tools to the nervous system, two U.S. scientists were doing the same at Washington University in St. Louis. They were Joseph Erlanger and Herbert Spencer Gasser, and they, too, concentrated on the impulses of single nerve axons in a successful search for some more fundamental knowledge of how the nervous system works.

Erlanger and Gasser discovered that the diameter of an axon determines the exact speed of impulses moving along the infinitesimally slender fiber. The larger the axon, they found, the faster its impulses travel, and vice versa. In a system where billions of fibers make up the message-carrying circuits, the impulse speed can play an important role. It determines the timing of message arrivals at various points fed by the unimaginably complicated communication lines of the brain, spinal cord, and nerves. The St. Louis scientists went on to find that the natural sizes of nerve fibers were somehow adapted to the jobs they were assigned. Where muscular action is often needed in a hurry the messages activating the contractions travel over motor fibers that are comparatively large. Messages of pain, however, are not moved as fast around the nervous system, so the fibers for this job are relatively small.

The two scientists from Washington University had again made extremely basic discoveries for understanding how nervous systems control life and thought. In 1944 they also received the Nobel Prize in Physiology or Medicine.

The foundations of still another Nobel Prize for work on the nerve cell was laid at a Long Island, New York, conference in 1937 by a British biologist, J. Z. Young. He pointed out that the shellfish, the squid, had a large, single axon running through its body. The fiber was large enough to be a nerve containing a whole bundle of axons, but Young assured his listeners that it was a single axon from a single cell body. He proposed that its unusual size offered an unprecedented opportunity to study the cell's functions, and thereby to learn about all nerve cells.

The fiber became known as the *squid giant axon*. It was hardly a giant with its tiny diameter of .03937 inch, but the dimensions were great compared to the largest human nerve fiber of about .0003937-inch diameter. Regardless, Young was right about the research potential of the giant axon, and in a few months it was the subject of study at Plymouth, England, and Woods Hole, Massachusetts. Both places were sites of marine biological laboratories, and squid were plentiful in the nearby waters of the Atlantic.

Scientists at these laboratories found that after a giant axon was carefully removed from a live squid and immersed in a small seawater bath it would still conduct nerve impulses when stimulated by a tiny shock or other means. In fact, it would continue responding to stimuli for many hours. The investigators

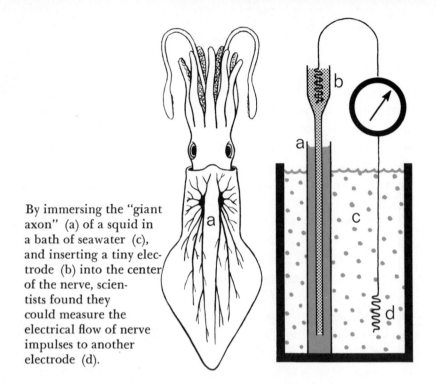

By immersing the "giant axon" (a) of a squid in a bath of seawater (c), and inserting a tiny electrode (b) into the center of the nerve, scientists found they could measure the electrical flow of nerve impulses to another electrode (d).

also found they could insert an extremely slender metal electrode inside the functioning axon to pick up internal electrical values. This allowed the Plymouth and Woods Hole scientists to test an important theory that had been around, but unprovable, since 1902.

That year a German physiologist, Julius Bernstein, had proposed the *membrane theory* for cells. He had decided that at rest (when no impulse was being conducted) a living nerve cell had the capability of producing a flow of electricity, as does a battery before its terminals are connected. Bernstein's theory suggested that the cell's electrical potential could be picked up if tiny enough electrodes from a sensitive enough galvanometer could be placed—one on the inside and one on the outside of the cell's surface membrane. If he were right the meter would register a small voltage (which is the measure of an electrical potential).

The membrane theory further indicated that in the brief moment when a cell conducted a nerve impulse an electrical current would momentarily flow across the cell membrane. The

52

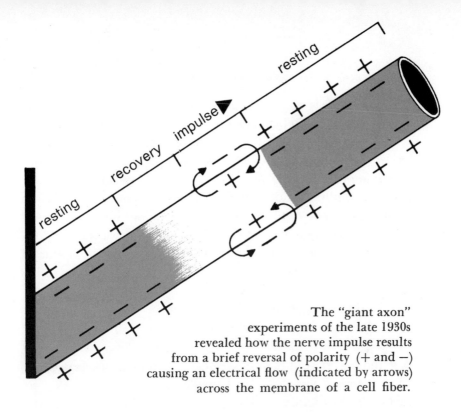

The "giant axon"
experiments of the late 1930s
revealed how the nerve impulse results
from a brief reversal of polarity (+ and −)
causing an electrical flow (indicated by arrows)
across the membrane of a cell fiber.

action, in a sense, would be powered by the pent-up electrical potential existing in the cell's resting stage. This brief electrical activity would occur from point to point on the axon as the impulse was conducted along its length. Bernstein's theory proposed that the impulsive burst of activity occurred when something like little gates in the membrane opened up to permit electrically charged particles, or *ions,* to pass between the inside and outside of the axon. The ionic flow would be the basis for a flow of electric current.

The theory, incidentally, would explain the relative slowness of the nerve impulse revealed by Helmholtz a half-century earlier. According to Bernstein's proposal, nerve electricity traveled across the membrane at right angles to the fiber as well as parallel to the axon. He assumed that an impulse acting at any given point on an axon automatically stimulated action in the immediately adjacent point. Thus the impulse sort of pushed itself along a fiber, and it moved much more slowly than would a direct, even flow of electricity in a wire.

53

These ideas were not provable, however, until electrical measurements could be made between the inside and outside of a cell. If the theory were right a small, brief electric current would be detectable flowing through any given point of the membrane as an impulse passed. But how could such measurements be made within the microscopic confines of a nerve cell? They simply couldn't—until the squid giant axon was recognized. Then it suddenly appeared that the membrane theory could be tested; the size of the squid fiber offered the opportunity to make electrical measurements between the alternate sides of a cell's surface membrane.

During the summer of 1939 four men, two on each side of the Atlantic, made history in the neurological sciences with comparable experiments on the giant axon. The work showed that the 37-year-old membrane theory could be checked upon. The scientists were A. L. Hodgkin and A. F. Huxley at Plymouth, England, and Kenneth S. Cole and Howard J. Curtis at Woods Hole, Massachusetts. Their experimentation was the beginning of a long series of studies of the cell membrane at rest and in action with nerve impulses.

The results showed that Bernstein was essentially correct, although he was not right about all that he proposed for the membrane theory. The studies of the giant axon on the shores of the Atlantic added immensely to the functional knowledge of the nerve cell. For their contributions Hodgkin and Huxley were each awarded one of the three shares in the Nobel Prize of 1963.

The third recipient of the same prize was John C. Eccles whose work at laboratories in New Zealand and Australia was also important to the developing knowledge of the neuron. Eccles and his associates used an ingenious technique to get electrodes inside single nerve cells while they were functioning in the brain tissue of live animals. Thus the scientists were able to study neurons at work in their natural environment along with other neurons. This allowed investigation of functions impossible to study with squid axons which had been removed from the animals.

The Eccles group studied individual neurons mostly in the brains of anesthetized cats. To find and break through a single cell (far, far smaller than the big squid cell) they used some newly developed electrodes, called *micropipettes*. They were hollow glass rods with tips so small in diameter that they required a microscope to see them. The centers were filled with a salt solution that conducted electricity from their points back to metal connections at the opposite ends of the tiny rods. Each was inserted into a cat's brain until the microscopic glass point impaled a single cell. The scientists could tell exactly when a cell was broken into by watching an oscilloscope registering the various electrical activities being detected by the micropipette as it moved into the brain tissue.

Eccles and his co-workers concentrated in particular on what happened electrically at the synapse, the junction between nerve cells. By applying their delicate technique with great skill and patience they recorded the internal electrical activity of many neurons to learn how each was influenced by impulses operating across the synapses. The work explained a great deal about the neuron-to-neuron communication in the most complex of all communication systems—the brain. The results were fundamentally important enough for Eccles to be included with Hodgkin and Huxley for the 1963 Nobel Prize.

By this time the electrical nature of the nerve cell was well established, but the underlying causes remained a mystery for they were mostly hidden somewhere in the chemical functions of the neuron. This became the most difficult area for exploration by the modern neurological scientist, although intensive studies of nerve chemistry (neurochemistry) had been conducted for nearly a half-century.

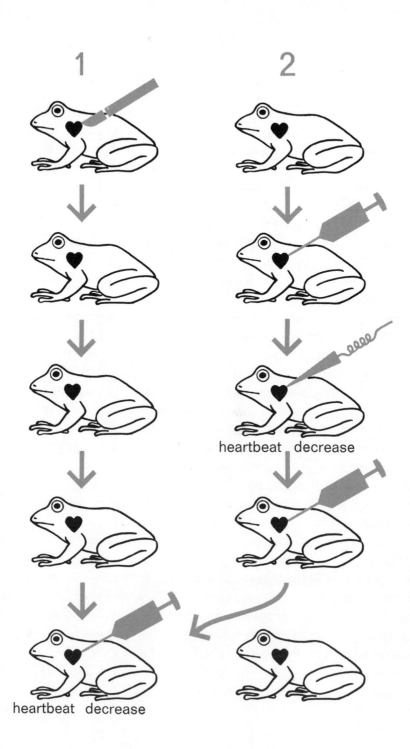

heartbeat decrease

heartbeat decrease

Loewi's classic experiment.

6 Chemistry and Nerve Messages

MOST MODERN research in neurochemistry goes back to a classic experiment conducted on two frog hearts in the 1920s. It was the work of Otto Loewi, an Austrian physiologist who also became a Nobel Prize winner.

Before Loewi's time most scientists had assumed that nerve impulses were transmitted from one cell to another by direct electrical transmission. They felt that the synapse between cells, or between cells and muscles, was like a splice between two wires, with the electricity flowing directly through the junction. A few scientists, however, had questioned this widely accepted idea. They suspected that the junction between cells was more complicated than a simple electrical contact. In fact, they had some indications that the synaptic transmission of impulses might be involved with a chemical process.

They were proven right by Loewi's classic experiment. He claimed that the idea for the experiment came to him at 3:00 A.M. during a sleepless night in 1921. He wrote down his thoughts, but the next morning couldn't read his own handwriting or remember what it was all about. Fortunately the idea came back to him the following night. This time he promptly left his bed for his laboratory to perform the experiment.

It was conducted upon two live frogs' hearts (for convenience sake we will label them *one* and *two*). On heart one Loewi severed the vagus nerve whose impulses reduce the heartbeat whenever the nerve is stimulated. He left the vagus nerve of heart two intact, but he injected the tiny organ with a small portion of a harmless liquid (Ringer's solution). Next he stimulated heart two's vagus nerve with a feeble electric shock, and the beat decreased. Then Loewi drew off a little of the Ringer's solution from heart two and injected it into heart one. As he suspected, it reduced the beat of heart one, just as if the vagus nerve had been stimulated before it was severed.

What did the test prove? It clearly indicated that a chemical had been introduced into heart two by action of the intact vagus nerve. Some of the chemical had mixed with the Ringer's solution and was carried over to heart one causing a reduction in its beat. From these results Loewi deduced that the actual transmission from a nerve cell is chemical rather than electrical.

Loewi could not identify the chemical so he simply called it *vagusstoff* (vagus material). Later he guessed that it might be a substance called *acetylcholine* that had been isolated in 1914 by the English biologist Henry H. Dale at the National Institute for Medical Research in London. But Loewi could not prove that vagusstoff was acetylcholine. In fact no one at the time could even say that the chemical existed in animals. Dale had found it in ergot, a fungus.

However, the English biologist had made a revealing discovery about acetylcholine. He had applied some to muscles where they connected with nerves and found that it caused a muscular contraction, the same as if he had stimulated the nerve with a light shock. This had led Dale to think that the chemical might be found in animals and that it might have something to do with nerve-muscle functions.

About a decade later Loewi's classic experiment came to Dale's attention, and it led him to follow up his earlier interest in acetylcholine. First he ascertained that it existed in animals. One day he and an associate collected the spleens of twenty-four horses killed at a local slaughterhouse, and through a difficult laboratory process they found that the spleens contained 334 milligrams (thousandths of a gram) of acetylcholine.

Knowing that the substance existed in animals, Dale and his

co-workers set up a series of intricate experiments to learn if it was released by motor nerves in the control of muscles. The English scientists used nerve-muscle preparations from cats' tongues and the legs of cats, dogs, and frogs. In each test the nerves were stimulated repeatedly by an electrical device that caused the related muscles to twitch with each stimulus. The muscles were then analyzed by an ingenious process to see if they had picked up acetylcholine from the nervous action. The difficulty of the search was later illustrated by Dale when he pointed out that a single nerve impulse released only .0000000000000001 gram of acetylcholine. Nevertheless, enough of the substance was located in the muscles so the English scientist was assured that synaptic action at nerve-muscle junctions released acetylcholine. The evidence indicated that the substance was related to transmission of the nerve impulse.

Acetylcholine became the first and best known *transmitter substance* of the nervous system. Subsequently a few other chemicals were either identified as or suspected to be transmitter substances. It is now thought that still other substances will be identified. Each transmitter appears to have its own work sites in the nervous system, and it deals with functions different from those of the other transmitters.

For opening up this field of study Loewi and Dale were jointly honored with the Nobel Prize for Physiology or Medicine in 1936. They had made one of the greatest breakthroughs of all in the neurological sciences.

From these dramatic beginnings scientists continued studying the activity at synapses, and they gradually pieced together evidence of what happens when a nerve impulse is transmitted across the junction. In overly simple terms it goes like this:

The electrical action conducted along an axon to a synapse causes the transmitter substance to be released into the ultra-narrow gap (the *synaptic cleft*) that separates the sending and

59

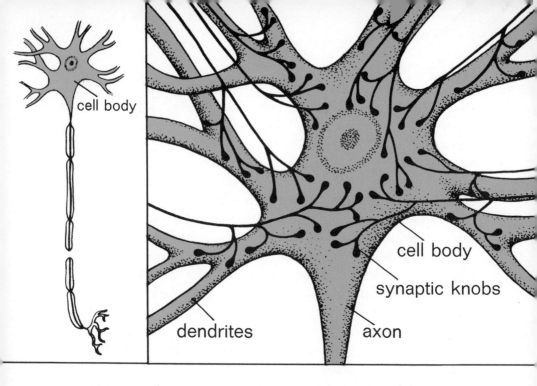

cell body

cell body

synaptic knobs

dendrites   axon

The body of a nerve cell and its dendrites are often contacted by axons (and their branchings) from many other cells. The actual contact of an axon is made through a "synaptic knob" that contains the

receiving cells. The chemical stimulates the receiving cell into action, and it in turn conducts an impulse.

But there are important variations on this synaptic process. Sometimes the released chemical simply increases the chance for an impulse to fire off in the receiving cell, but it actually doesn't happen. However, the action establishes a condition that makes the receiving cell more easily forced into activity by impulses that may arrive over other synapses from other cells. And then there are instances where the chemical arriving at the synaptic cleft actually reduces the chances for causing the receiving cell to fire an impulse.

The complexity of all this chemical interaction of cells in the brain is practically beyond comprehension. One is absolutely baffled at the thought that the organ has billions and billions of

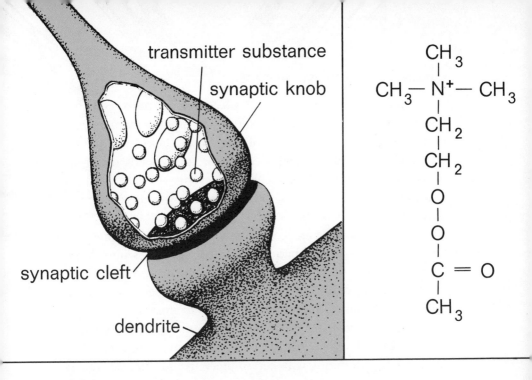

chemical for transmitting nerve impulses across a minute "synaptic cleft." The chemical formula for the best known chemical transmitter, acetylcholine, appears at upper right.

neurons, each making many synaptic connections with neighboring cells, which in turn make many more junctions with other neighbors. Then all of these junctions are sites for continual chemical activities having various effects upon the brain's cell-to-cell communication. No wonder that brain tissue has been aptly described as the most complicated material in the universe.

In 1970 three scientists who had been struggling with these complexities for many years were awarded the Nobel Prize. Each had made major contributions to our understanding of transmitter substances and the mechanics of their use in the nervous system. The award winners were Julius Axelrod of the National Institute of Mental Health, Bethesda, Maryland; Ulf von Euler of the Karolinska Institute in Stockholm; and Sir Bernard Katz of University College in London.

61

The advancing chemical knowledge of the nerve cell that flowed from the Loewi-Dale breakthrough brought many important changes to man's view of the brain. Scientists quickly recognized that to function well the organ depends upon the proper performance of tiny chemical events constantly taking place at billions of synapses. When this chemistry is changed, it alters the workings of the brain.

In turn, scientists recognized that the synaptic processes can be changed for good or bad by chemical influences introduced into the nervous system in various ways, such as through food or drink, or an injection. This understanding provided new insights into the brain and nerves. Here are a few examples.

The mind altering drugs, from LSD discovered in 1943 to tranquillizers developed in the 1950s, are thought to exert their influence by interfering with certain nerve transmitter substances and the chemical process in which they work. Thus the brain's normal electrical activity is changed with results ranging from utter psychological calm to wild hallucinations.

The new brain chemistry helped explain some old and mysterious sources of damage for the nervous system. For example, the long-dreaded disease of botulism, associated with poorly canned or sealed food, was explained in terms of nerve chemistry in 1949. The villain, botulinus toxin, prevents the release of acetylcholine at the junction of nerves and muscles. The victims suffer mainly from muscular paralysis, and often die from respiratory failure.

Dreadful nerve gases, Tabun and Sarin, were developed by the Germans in World War II and manufactured in industrial lots. Very small quantities can deal a rapid, horrible death to a victim. The gases literally wreck the chemical processes involving acetylcholine, and the normal controls of the nervous system are knocked out. Fortunately the gases were never used. When the U.S. Army wanted to dispose of its nerve gas in recent years it became a difficult, dangerous job.

Parkinson's disease, one of the cruelest disorders of the nervous system, became better understood because of increasing knowledge of nerve chemistry. It is now believed that the disease results from a certain chemical imbalance in transmission of nerve impulses. In the 1960s it was found that a drug called *L-Dopa* can often restore the lost chemical balance, and patients treated with it often improve dramatically.

The neurons, the most perplexing of living cells, continue to hold some of our greatest scientific challenges, and many must be met through increasing our knowledge of the chemistry of the nervous system.

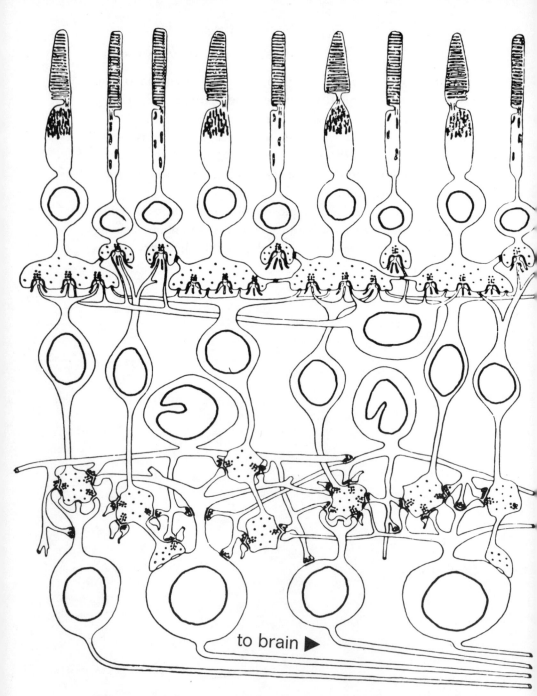

The complex interconnections of only nine of the thousands upon thousands of receptor cells in a primate retina are shown here, to suggest the incredible complexity of the eye.

7 Knowledgeable Neurons

As SCIENTISTS developed an understanding of the neuron, an oversimplified description of the cell might portray it as both a battery and a switch. Using its own electricity, the cell is either "switched" on or off, conducting or not conducting a nerve impulse. The great complexities of the nerve cell would thus seem to lie in its vast numbers and connections. But scientific investigations of recent years began to reveal that this unit, which Cajal considered the aristocrat of all cells, was in itself much more sophisticated than early studies had indicated. Indeed, some modern research might lead one to believe that individual nerve cells might harbor some thinking power of their own.

In 1959 a classic scientific paper was published with the unusual title, "What the Frog's Eye Tells the Frog's Brain." It reported on studies conducted at the Massachusetts Institute of Technology (M.I.T.) by four scientists, J. Y. Lettvin, H. R. Maturana, W. S. McCulloch, and W. H. Pitts.

The scientists investigated the frog's optic nerve leading from behind the retina of the eye back to the brain. One of the M.I.T. team had already determined that this tiny nerve contained about a half-million fibers each of which was the axon of a nerve cell. In many, many frogs the M.I.T. investigators meticulously explored the nature of this minute bundle of fibers behind a living, functioning eye by probing into individual fibers with an extremely fine, platinum-tipped microelectrode. When the tiny probe impaled a fiber, it picked up whatever nerve impulses were set off in the axon by visual stimuli in the eye, which had been trained on carefully arranged images in front of

65

the animal. The scientists then compared the impulses and the incoming visual images to see if they could figure out what kind of messages the eye was actually sending the brain.

Prior to the M.I.T. studies, it was easy to assume that the eye was sort of a TV camera transmitting pictures back to the brain, or "the mind's eye," where they were analyzed. But the frog's eye experiments indicated that actually the cells of the eye and optic nerve are literally an extension of the brain, and at least some of the picture analysis is handled as the visual information is conveyed back to the brain. Thus it appeared that these neurons are more than simple information carriers; they are, in a way, censors of what the frog's eye tells his brain.

This was evident when the M.I.T. scientists determined that the fibers bundled into the tiny optic nerve did not all react the same as various images were presented to the frog's eye. In fact, the researchers decided that the bundle had at least four different kinds of cell fibers, each of which had a task tailor-made to the basic needs of a frog.

One of the most interesting of these cell fibers tempted the scientists to call them "bug perceivers." They did not conduct impulses unless a black dot entered the visual field of the frog's eye. The fiber would continue to fire off impulses as long as the dot remained in view, but it would cease when the dot left the visual field. If a pattern of many dots was moved in front of the eye these dot-perceiving fibers did not react—unless the movement of one of the dots was different from all the others. It seemed obvious that here were highly specialized nerve cells designed to aid the frog in detecting one of his main dietary staples when it flew by.

The scientists further explored this assumption by having a frog's eye see a color photograph of a small scene typical of the creature's habitat. The "bug-perceiver" cells did not react to the picture alone; however, they did fire when a small speck was moved across the scene. But then they ceased reacting if the

66

speck was stuck to a point on the picture, and the entire image was moved. Thus the bug-perceivers were hard to fool. They refused to tell the frog's brain about anything other than a small object, like a fly, moving against the scenery.

Other fibers reacted only when a sharp edge contrasting with the visual background moved into the visual field of the animal eye. They continued firing as long as the edge was in view, either moving or stationary. Still other neuronal fibers were only interested in moving edges, and when an edge stopped, the cells ceased firing. And finally the scientists recognized cells that fired impulses only when the light entering the eye was reduced. They would electrically react, for example, when a shadow darkened whatever the frog was looking at.

While the M.I.T. scientists were reporting their results, two physiologists at the Harvard Medical School were studying the visual systems of cats with results that strengthened the idea of individual nerve cells having specialized jobs. D. H. Hubel and T. N. Wiesel used fine microelectrodes to tap single neurons of cats' brains in an area of the organ associated with vision. Each cat in the experiment was anesthetized, and its head was fixed so the eyes, still functioning, were trained on a screen. As the Harvard scientists projected various images on the screen, they observed their test instruments to see what happened electrically to each of the particular neurons impaled by a microelectrode inserted into the exposed brain.

As in the M.I.T. studies, Hubel and Wiesel found that individual brain cells seemed to specialize in handling only certain jobs as visual data arrived from a cat's eyes. The investigators usually projected bars of light on the screen. Some of the cells being studied would fire off impulses only when a bar of light was tilted at a certain angle. When it was tilted to another angle, the cell ceased firing. Other neurons reacted only to something moving across the screen in one specific direction. With a change in direction the cell stopped firing.

The marvelously specialized neurological mechanisms of the frog are relatively simple compared to

the more sophisticated mechanisms of the cat, whose larger brain size accommodates the complexities.

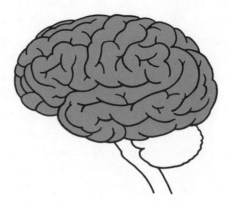

The human brain, which regulates the most complicated of all living systems, reflects the fact in its greater size.

These and numerous other findings about particular brain cells in cats indicated that their brains utilized a much more complex system for visual data processing than the frog's brain—which, of course, stands to reason. And in this more sophisticated system, it was evident that individual neurons had very specific jobs to do in helping cats deal with what they see.

Still other modern scientists with other creatures encountered the same kind of evidence indicating that nerve cells are not limited to the simple transmission of nerve messages, but are filters, in a sense, accepting some messages and rejecting others. At the California Institute of Technology Cornelius A. G. Wiersma found this kind of specialization in the nervous systems of crayfish. One of the most fascinating of the crayfish's neurons fires only when light enters the creature's eye from the sky. If a crayfish is turned upside down the cell still limits its electrical action to light from the sky. The cell appears to be conscious of gravity and refuses to operate except for light coming from a direction opposite the pull of gravity.

These neurons, which literally seem to exhibit a degree of intelligence, emphasize how tremendous the capabilities of the human brain are with its twelve billion tiny servants of life and thought, if each cell or group of cells is designed to cope with very specific jobs. They also emphasize what a tremendous puzzle scientific explorers of the brain face as they try to figure out all the marvelous and mysterious capabilities of the inner space of the human head.

8 Memory: The Great Frontier

IN ESSENCE the brain is a machine that remembers. Its billions of neurons form a marvelous, mysterious memory bank that serves and molds a person in every moment of life.

The neurons not only remember the common experiences of today and yesterday, they also hold ancestral memories carried genetically from the earliest life on earth. They keep the timing of the heartbeat, the temperature of the body, and many other regulatory functions of the living organism. These ancient memories also guide our deepest drives for self-preservation and the continuance of the human race. They retain old likes and dislikes that make us fear the dark and seek the light, or jump back at the sight of a snake or stop to listen to the rhythmical beat of a drum. In short, our memories are the mix of human behavior—pleasure, rage, love, hate, trust, distrust, fight, and flight—and they are seated in the least known recesses of the neurons characterized as the mind.

But what is memory? Where and how does it occur in the brain? These questions mark off the leading frontier of modern brain research. If they are answered some of the greatest mysteries of the nervous system will be solved.

Over the ages great thinkers often concluded that in some small way a memory makes a physical mark in the brain. In the seventeenth century René Descartes spoke of the brain having "traces" of the things it remembered. Early this century a French scientist, Richard Semon, named the trace, whatever it is, the *engram*. Today's scientists continue trying to find and define the engram, for they still believe that a memory leaves its mark among the neurons.

71

In recent decades many provocative experiments have indicated that the mind certainly has a physical basis that can be influenced physically. This has been evident in modern research with electrical stimulation of the brain (ESB), the technique developed in the last century by Gustav Fritsch and Eduard Hitzig.

In 1949 the Nobel Prize was awarded to Walter Rudolf Hess, a Swiss scientist, for some amazing research on areas deep in the brains of cats. With the creatures anesthetized, Hess inserted fine wires through their skulls into carefully chosen brain sites. When they were conscious again, Hess could drastically alter the cats' emotional behavior by transmitting a small, gentle electric current into their brains. He explained one such change as follows:

"Even a formerly good-natured cat turns bad-tempered; it starts to spit and, when approached, launches a well-aimed attack. As the pupils [of the eyes] simultaneously dilate widely and the hair bristles, a picture develops such as is shown by the cat if a dog attacks it while it cannot escape."

With many such experiments, Hess found that he could stimulate various emotions. It was a major research milestone because the Swiss scientist had revealed that emotions were not as obscure as they were thought to be; they might be explained in physical terms.

Other scientists continued the exploration and confirmed that animal behavior could be related to electrical processes that an engineer might understand. For example, at the University of Michigan, James Olds found that rats had "pleasure centers" deep in their brains. When the area was stimulated electrically, it made the rat experience a tremendous sense of pleasure. In fact, Olds arranged for rats to stimulate their own pleasure centers by touching a small foot pedal that would cause a minute current to enter the animal's wired-up brain. Once an animal discovered the pedal, he might push it as many as five thousand times an hour for the pleasure it gave him.

72

As Hess, Olds, and others were making such basic discoveries about animal brains, a famous Montreal brain surgeon, Wilder Penfield, was reporting on some astonishing work with human patients. First it should be noted that when Penfield operated on a person's brain for medical reasons, he only needed to anesthetize a small area of the scalp and skull so he could fashion a trap door from the skin and bone to expose the underlying gray matter in the general area where surgery was required. Since the brain suffers no pain, it required no anesthesia; therefore the patient could always remain conscious during the entire procedure. To determine precisely what brain area served what purpose, Penfield stimulated the wrinkled surface, or cortex, with tiny electric currents as he watched or listened for responses from the patient. These explorations, conducted on hundreds of patients, produced some amazing results.

One time, for example, the surgeon was operating on a fourteen-year-old girl in an attempt to prevent epileptic seizures. As he stimulated a certain area of the brain with his electrodes, the girl cried out, "Oh, I can see something come at me!" As the electrical stimulus was removed and reapplied, it caused the child's fear to subside, but then return. She heard voices yelling at her and decided they were her brothers and her mother calling to her as they did in the past.

"Oh, there it goes," said the patient on the operating table, "everybody is yelling!" The electrode was lifted and moved slightly to another point. "Something dreadful is going to happen," cried the girl. "There they go, yelling at me; stop them!"

In similar fashion other surgical patients over the years had memories triggered by Penfield's gentle electric brain stimuli. A number of people heard familiar music, and some could keep time with the tunes by tapping the side of the operating table. A South African heard his friends laughing and talking back home. Electrical stimulation made a mother feel she was in the past in

73

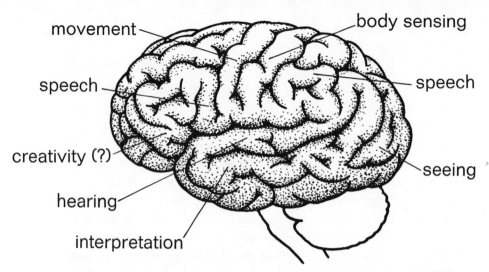

movement · body sensing · speech · speech · creativity (?) · seeing · hearing · interpretation

The famous Montreal neurosurgeon, Wilder Penfield, precisely mapped many human brain functions by electrical stimulation of the exposed brains of patients.

her kitchen listening to her son Frankie playing outside. She could even hear the familiar neighborhood sounds that she had listened to years ago.

Penfield and his colleagues were fascinated by the way he could pull memories from the brain with the touch of an electrode. Each remembrance seemed to play out its scenes like a short movie film. If the surgeon lifted his electrode, the film would stop. Put it down on the brain once more, and the presentation would start again from the beginning. But what are the films and where are they stored? Penfield or others have never been able to explain.

As electronic equipment became smaller and lighter, it added a new dimension to ESB techniques. Tiny radio receivers that could be easily carried by animal or human subjects allowed scientists to deliver brain stimuli from a distance by remote control. Now, animals uninhibited by wires could be stimulated as they roamed freely with their fellow creatures, and the scientist could observe the effects of the emotion-changing brain stimuli in a natural setting.

The most publicized of such experiments were conducted by

74

a Spanish-born scientist at Yale University, José Delgado. For example, he wired up the brain of an aggressive, tough monkey that was the boss of a colony of monkeys. The boss could command the most food, space, and everything he wanted in the animals' cage, but when Delgado radioed a stimulus to a certain area of the boss monkey's brain, its aggressiveness disappeared, and its little empire fell apart. The other monkeys recognized the change, and their old boss soon became just one of the common tribe. However, when Delgado shut off the radio-controlled stimuli, the boss turned nasty again and in a few minutes was back firmly in control of his caged realm.

The scientist once demonstrated his great faith in his technique of remote brain stimulation. Back home in Spain he wired up the brain of a brave bull, and then, in a bull ring, Delgado, playing the role of a toreador, allowed the fierce animal to charge him. When the oncoming bull was only a few feet away, the scientist pressed a button on a small radio transmitter in his hand. The signal activated an electrode in the bull's brain, and the beast suddenly lost its forward drive. Whatever made it a fierce, enraged creature was abruptly subdued, and the animal, becoming a friendly Ferdinand the Bull, walked calmly away from the scientist.

With these and numerous other experiments, Delgado stirred up public fears of widespread brain control. The work prompted visions of all of our heads being wired and controlled from some central point, making robots out of otherwise unpredictable human beings. But we're far from understanding the brain enough to make such control very effective, even if someone tried to get away with it. Delgado refused to worry about the idea; he was more concerned with the use of ESB as a tool for learning about the basic functions of the brain.

But while ESB on animals and humans might help pinpoint where certain memories lie in the brain, it still offered no explanation of exactly what happens when a memory is lodged among the neurons. What kind of a "trace" does it leave? What is the engram?

From the 1920s to about 1950 a well-known American scientist, Karl S. Lashley, devoted practically his entire career to the search for the engram. His subjects were rats, and his experiments generally went like this: A rat was trained in some simple task. It was then anesthetized, and a tiny, carefully selected portion of its brain was removed. After recovery from the operation, the animal was tested to see if the learning had also been removed by the brain surgery. Lashley performed the experiment on thousands of rats, removing different parts of their brains hoping to find, by the process of elimination, where the memory from the training went.

In 1950 Lashley wrote that all of his research revealed a lot about "what and where the memory trace is not," but nothing of what it is or where it goes. The scientist added with a touch of wit that his piles of data sometimes left the impression "that learning just is not possible."

Right after this, in the 1950s, a group of scientists at the University of California at Berkeley began some remarkable studies of rat brains and learning. The group (David Krech, Mark R. Rosenzweig, Edward L. Bennett, and Marian C. Diamond) worked with many, many pairs of rats selected for being very much alike. Soon after weaning, the baby rats in each pair were separated. One was confined alone in a small dark cage in a quiet room. It was comfortable and well fed, but it had absolutely nothing to do. The second rat was allowed to live in a large, bright cage with other such animals. They had many toys, ladders, wheels, and boxes, and they were taken out daily by a trainer to explore a special area of the room. Of course this more fortunate rat of the pair learned a great deal more in life than the brother rat confined to the small cage.

On the eightieth day both animals were killed, and their brains were thoroughly analyzed and compared. There were telling differences. The active rats, for example, generally had a heavier cortex (the outer surface of the brain) than the confined rats. When the researchers looked at the neurons of the two brains with an electron microscope, they noted that the cells of the active rat were larger than those in the confined animal. These and other differences between the two types of rat brains indicated that learning did have a physical impact on the rat brain, but the California scientists remained cautious about drawing such a flat conclusion. They recognized that because of the brain's extreme complexity many factors other than memory might have caused the differences in their rats' brains.

Back again in the 1950s scientists began thinking of another way to get at the mysteries of memory. It was suggested that the elusive engram might actually be changes in certain molecules within the neurons, and by the 1960s a large number of studies were investigating the molecular basis of memory.

For a number of years there were two leading candidates for the "memory molecule": protein and one of the nucleic acids, RNA (ribonucleic acid) which had been associated with the genetic processes of heredity. Proteins were once described as "the principal stuff of life," and the nucleic acids as "its blueprint—the molecules on which the Secret of Life . . . is written."

First of all, some scientists theorized that in addition to its known role in genetics, RNA might also serve as the memory molecule. One of the proponents was a Swedish scientist, Holger Hydén. He and a colleague, Jan-Erik Edström, developed some remarkable techniques using small mammals to study the relationship of RNA and neurons. They devised some astonishing methods for removing single cells from the animal brains so they could extract and measure their unbelievably small quantities of RNA. These experiments provided evidence that of all cells the neurons contain more RNA than any.

Hydén and another scientist, E. Egyházi, then set out to find

77

if learning would increase the cell's RNA even more. They worked with two groups of rats. The animals of one group were forced to learn how to walk up a slanting tightwire to obtain food on a shelf. It was a difficult learning task that took several days. The second group of animals simply received the food without having to climb for it. Thus in the end the scientists had two batches of rats, one with the learning, one without.

The creatures were then killed, and their brain cells were analyzed for RNA. The trained rats' cells now had more than the untrained rats'. The results suggested that memories from the learning process had been laid down in the brain by the addition of RNA. But this was far from conclusive, and the chance for error and misinterpretation was great. After all Hydén and his associates were dealing with micromicrograms of RNA, a millionth of a millionth of a gram.

A number of complicated experiments in the 1960s also tried to find out if protein was the memory molecule. In general this research was a matter of training animals and subsequently trying to determine if the resulting memory could be erased by injecting the brain with a substance known to interfere with protein synthesis. These studies, as with the RNA experiments, produced some provocative results, but they were also far from conclusive.

In all the searches for the memory molecule, the most dramatic were a number of experiments using a technique called *memory transfer*. The idea, which became extremely controversial, was simply to transfer certain substances from a trained brain to an untrained brain and thus transfer the learning.

The origin of the idea seems to go back to the 1950s when two Texas graduate students, James V. McConnell and Robert Thompson, were experimenting with the common flatworm and concluded that the animal, despite an ultra-simple brain, could be trained to do some very simple things—like crawling toward a light to avoid receiving an electric shock that would be adminis-

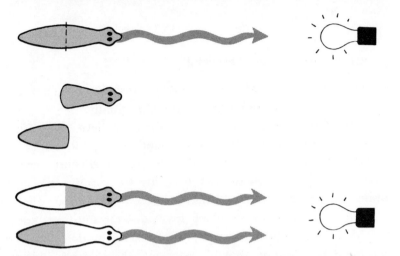

McConnell's flatworm experiments indicated that when a worm trained to crawl toward a light was cut in two, the memory was somehow transferred to the newly formed brain of the animal that grew from the tail.

tered if the creature failed to make the desired move. Subsequently McConnell went to the University of Michigan where he set up a special laboratory and conducted some fascinating memory-transfer experiments with trained flatworms.

For this research he depended on a basic feature of the animals. If cut in two, one worm becomes two complete worms. The head end with the brain grows a tail, and the tail end grows a head with a new brain—all in about thirty days. Indeed, starting with one animal, and dividing and subdividing it, the pieces can be regenerated into as many as fifty complete worms, each with a brain and tail. Using this unusual capability, McConnell trained some worms, then cut them in two. Surprisingly, the tail ends, once they had developed their new brains, exhibited the same training as the original animals. Furthermore, the scientist found he could continue dividing up a single flatworm, and each new brain would provide its regenerated body with a significant amount of the original training.

In an even more dramatic experiment McConnell used a cannibalistic species of flatworm. The scientist trained one group of the cannibals and fed them to an untrained group. After the

79

animals enjoyed their meal of learned worms, they turned out to have acquired the training denied them originally.

The flatworm results were hard to believe, but other scientists in numerous laboratories found they could duplicate the work. However, McConnell's results remained controversial. Critics particularly questioned that his flatworms were ever trained in the first place, and they refused to accept the validity of his testing methods, on which his transfer results depended. The Michigan scientist, however, refused to be put down, and he continued to maintain that his research offered good evidence that the tiny memories of a flatworm were transferable.

During the late 1960s and early 1970s numerous reports came from around the nation and around the world about memory transfer experiments using rats instead of worms. In these cases brain tissue or RNA was removed from the brains of trained rats and injected into the brains of untrained animals. The most publicized, and most controversial, of the experiments were conducted at the University of California, Los Angeles, where investigators claimed they had been able to transfer learning by transferring RNA from a trained to an untrained rat. A number of prominent scientists denounced the results, but then some of them changed their minds and praised the findings.

As these and other sophisticated kinds of experiments continue, scientists pretty much agree that the most exclusive secrets of life and thought are definitely to be found on the molecular level in the depths of individual neurons. However, the barrier on this greatly confined frontier of the brain is its unimaginable *complication.* Other sciences dealing with such complex matters as travel through outer space are complicated, but none compare with the immense, involved complexities of inner space, which must be overcome as scientists explore the brain.

Who are we? How do we relate to the world around us? These are questions to be answered only by this momentous science of man's brain trying to understand itself.

References

ADRIAN, EDGAR D.: "The Activity of Nerve Fibres." Nobel Lecture, December 12, 1932.

ASIMOV, ISAAC: *Asimov's Biographical Encyclopedia of Science and Technology.* Garden City, N.Y.: Doubleday, 1964.

BRAZIER, MARY A. B.: *A History of the Electrical Activity of the Brain.* London: Pitman, 1961.

——: "The Evolution of Concepts Relating to the Electrical Activity of the Nervous System 1600 to 1800," from *The History and Philosophy of the Brain and Its Functions.* London: Anglo-American Symposium, 1957.

COLE, KENNETH S.: *Membranes, Ions and Impulses.* Los Angeles: University of Calif. Press, 1968.

DALE, HENRY H.: "Some Recent Extensions of the Chemical Transmission of the Effects of Nerve Impulses." Nobel Lecture, December 12, 1936.

ECCLES, JOHN C.: *The Physiology of Nerve Cells.* Baltimore: Johns Hopkins Press, 1957.

ERLANGER, JOSEPH: "Some Observations on the Responses of Single Nerve Fibers." Nobel Lecture, December 12, 1947.

FULTON, JOHN F., and HARVEY CUSHING: "A Bibliographical Study of the Galvani and the Aldini Writings on Animal Electricity," *Annals of Science,* 1936, 1: 241.

FULTON, JOHN F., and LEONARD G. WILSON: *Selected Readings in the History of Physiology,* 2nd Ed. Springfield, Ill.: C. C. Thomas, 1966.

GASSER, HERBERT S.: "Mammalian Nerve Fibers." Nobel Lecture, December 12, 1945.

HOGBEN, LANCELOT: *Science for the Citizen.* New York: Alfred A. Knopf, 1938.

KATZ, BERNARD: *Nerve, Muscle, and Synapse.* New York: McGraw Hill, 1966.

REFERENCES

LIDDELL, E. G. T.: *The Discovery of Reflexes*. Oxford at the Clarendon Press, 1960.

LOEWI, OTTO. "The Chemical Transmission of Nerve Action." Nobel Lecture, December 12, 1936.

RAMÓN Y CAJAL, S.: *Recollections of My Life*. Philadelphia, 1937.

STEVENS, LEONARD A.: *Explorers of the Brain*. New York: Alfred A. Knopf, 1971.

WALKER, W. CAMERON: "Animal Electricity Before Galvani," *Annals of Science*, 1937, 2: 84.

WOOLDRIDGE, DEAN E.: *The Machinery of the Brain*. New York: McGraw Hill, 1963.

Index

ABOUT THE AUTHOR

Leonard Stevens is the author of more than a dozen books for adults and young people and many national magazine articles. Mr. Stevens was born in Lisbon, New Hampshire. He holds B.A. and M.A. degrees from the State University of Iowa.

Before he became a writer, Mr. Stevens worked as a member of a ski patrol and as a radio news editor. During World War II, he served as a captain in the United States Air Force.

The author and his wife and their four children make their home in Bridgewater, Connecticut.

ABOUT THE ARTIST

Henry Roth is a photographer-painter. He has produced television commercials, and both produced and directed an educational film and a film for New York's Joffrey Ballet.

Mr. Roth was born in Cleveland, Ohio, and received his degree from the Cleveland Institute of Art. He now lives in New York City.

DATE DUE

O.gellott			